Additional Praise for

Meant to Be

"These wonderful stories remind us of the miracle that love is, and the magical ways it comes into our lives. *Meant to Be* proves that, at the deepest levels, destiny is always at work in our lives."

> —Susannah Seton, author of *Simple Pleasures* and
> *Simple Pleasures of the Home*

"*Chicken Soup* stories are delightful appetizers, but many of the stories in *Meant to Be* are a main course. You will be digesting these for a long time."

> —*Connection* magazine

"Few books make me cry, but this one did, many times. The best collection of heart-full stories that I have ever read!"

> —M. J. Ryan, author of *Attitudes of Gratitude*
> and editor of A *Grateful Heart*

Meant to Be

Meant to Be

Miraculous True Stories to Inspire a Lifetime of Love

ↂ

Compiled by
JOYCE & BARRY VISSELL

CONARI PRESS
Berkeley, California

The authors wish to thank the following for permission to reprint: "The Relationship That Started on the Rocks" by Bettine Clemen, reprinted by permission of the author from *Open Your Ears to Love,* ©1999, the Hovenden Press, Minneapolis, MN. "The Best Christmas Present" by Myrna L. Smith, reprinted by permission from *Expect Miracles* ©1999 by Mary Ellen, reprinted by permission of Conari Press.

Conari Press books are distributed by Publishers Group West
Cover photography © The Special Photographers Company / Photonica
Hand tinting by Peggy Lindt
Cover and book design by Claudia Smelser
Cover art direction by Ame Beanland

Library of Congress Cataloging-in-Publication Data

Vissell, Joyce.
Meant to be : miraculous true stories to inspire a lifetime of love /
Joyce & Barry Vissell.
p.   cm.
ISBN: 1-57324-161-X
1. Man-woman relationships.   2. Love.   I. Vissell, Barry.   II. Title.
HQ801.A3 V57 2000
306.7—dc21   99–045498

To our parents, who have shown us what it means to stay committed, smoothing the rough edges of a marriage over the years.

To all people everywhere, who have a magical, miraculous relationship story of their own, if they would simply look.

To all the contributors of this book, for sharing their gems with the world.

To the magic that runs through all of creation, and brings two people together in the sacred bond of love.

To all those who have felt peace and acceptance with their partner, and had the courage to say, "It was meant to be!"

Meant to Be

. . . .

Contents

True Love Miracles in Everyone

. . . .

From the beginning of our relationship in 1964, we have often felt the hands of destiny at work behind the scenes. Over the thirty-six years we have been together, we have learned to accept the miraculous happenings bringing us together as a couple, leading us through our trials, and strengthening our heart connection. So often have we thought about our relationship and used the words, "meant to be."

Naturally, we assumed there must be many others who felt the same way. At our workshops over the years, where we have shared many of the extraordinary happenings in our own relationship, we excitedly announced our plans to collect true stories for this book. We asked participants to share with us the miracles in their relationships. Inevitably, we were met with silent, blank, puzzled, and sometimes uncomfortable looks.

We soon realized that most people simply do not think of their relationships in terms of the miraculous, or they assume miracles happen to other people. If we were going to collect unbelievable stories, we were going to have to lovingly coax open the oysters and gently extract the pearls.

We decided to experiment on our eighty-year-old mothers, Helen Vissell and Louise Wollenberg. They have long been accustomed to our experimenting on them, beginning with the years when we were both in psychiatric training. We used to sit our parents down and, disregarding their groans of embarrassment, awkwardly query about their childhoods. This time, however, we each sat with our own mother, and gently pried, "There must be a miracle story about meeting or working things out with Dad."

Their initial response was, "Oh no, that's for other people," but there was something about the faraway look in their eyes that caused us to ask more and more questions. Finally, little by little, two gems emerged ("A Date To Remember" and "The Resolution"). Our experiment was a success!

So, believing that there is a miraculous love story within each person, we started coaxing out the pearls. What we uncovered is a complete buried treasure, a book full of amazingly precious gems that will bring joy to your heart, tears to your eyes, and inspiration to your relationships.

The stories in this book may be viewed by some as evidence of synchronicity, the ordered and purposeful way events in the universe relate, and the perfect timing of "coincidences." Or they may be viewed as spiritual or even angelic interventions in human happenings. Rather than trying to explain miracles, we prefer to simply appreciate the mystery of life and the awesome powers that guide our every step. Within each true story is a gem of love and wisdom from which we can all learn.

We hope these stories awaken in you a higher trust in the miraculous in human relationships. We also hope these stories inspire you to ask for help in your relationships, past, present, and future. You don't need to sit back and wait for a miracle. You have every right to ask for one. Not only ask, but open yourself to receive the loving guidance you are seeking.

Our greatest hope, through offering this collection of stories, is to inspire you to live more fully every moment, to love and appreciate now the ones with whom you are in relationship, rather than putting it off into the uncertain future. Being fully present in this life, making every day count, and living from the heart is a noble and worthy goal.

Miraculous Meetings

. . . .

ow two people are brought together has always remained a spiritual mystery. The following stories will not solve the mystery, but they will give you a feeling for the unseen forces at play behind all relationships. We believe there is a strong, mostly unseen, energy of love guiding us every step of our lives. This divine guidance brings us to the right relationship at the right time. The sometimes amazing stories in this first section show the magnitude and intelligence of this guiding power.

There is a destiny to two people joining into a committed relationship. What is ordinarily called "chemistry" between two people is really destiny at work. Two souls are drawn together to learn from each other. What seems like a crazy coincidence to some is to us the loving hand of guidance. Many times, people are guided to several or even a series of partners. Each of these relationships is *important and has been brought to each person lovingly for their highest growth. Some relationships have difficult lessons to teach, and when learned, there is the need to move on to learn new lessons from someone else. Sometimes the most difficult lesson is the peaceful acceptance of the need for transition, that a romantic relationship with a particular person is not in the best interest for either person.*

Some relationships contain all the lessons within the context of the one relationship. Our own relationship of thirty-six years has felt to us to be a series of mini-relationships. We went as far as we could go in one direction, experienced a mini-death or ending, and then the change of direction felt like a renewed commitment. We like the image of the mythical phoenix rising from the ashes, something beautiful being born after something of no more use has died, a beginning that can only arise from a proper ending.

True Love
. . . .

WHEN I WAS two years old, my mother put me in a day care center. She tells the story of how I was terrified to stay at this place until a two-year-old boy named Bobby joined the group. As long as Bobby was there, I was not afraid. Both of our mothers had to work full time, so Bobby and I were there every day together. The staff reported to my mother that we were never far from each other's side. When nap time came we would refuse to nap unless our blankets were side by side.

After three years in day care, it was time for public school kindergarten. The day care staff tried to prepare us for the fact that we wouldn't be together again. That didn't make sense to my five-year-old mind. I wanted to always be with Bobby.

Our mothers, acting independently of each other, enrolled us in the district's elementary school. Imagine our surprise when I reluctantly went for my first day of kindergarten and there was Bobby! We were in the same class! Again, we played together every day.

Bobby was the bright spot in my life, since my home life was anything but happy and secure. My father would go out drinking and come home and hit my mother. My only joy and security was my time with Bobby at school.

In first grade, the children started to tease us for playing together so much. We didn't care. Our favorite activity was swinging and telling each other jokes. We would laugh for a long time over our jokes.

Meanwhile, life at home was growing more and more unhappy. Lying in bed at night, I would hear my father yelling at my mother and my mother crying. I felt so sad I didn't know what to do. To comfort myself, I thought of Bobby during those times and tried to remember the jokes he'd told me that day.

In second and third grade the teasing grew intense. The boys called Bobby a sissy for playing with me. Sometimes he'd leave me and go off to play with the boys. Those were very sad days. Usually, though, he'd continue to play with me.

One night, when I was eight years old, my father came home more drunk than ever and began hitting my mother very hard. I tried to stop him and he struck at me. I ran to my room crying. I wished I could sneak out of my house and be with Bobby. In the middle of the night my mother woke me saying, "Get up, pack some of your favorite things. We are leaving here for good. Now hurry!"

My mother's voice was urgent and I obeyed her. We got in the car and drove west for seven days. All the time we were driving I cried. I wanted to be with Bobby, the one person that I felt secure and happy with.

I gradually adjusted to a new life in California. I never saw my father again. I learned to make new friends, yet every night for years I thought about Bobby and missed him. My mother would not let me write to him. She said my father could then find us and maybe kill her. That sounded pretty scary to me. Over the years, she refused to tell me about my past, even what city we had lived in. In time, I forgot all about Bobby.

I became a rebellious teenager and left home when I was sixteen. At seventeen, I married a man ten years older than me. I thought I loved this man until, shortly after we were married, I discovered he was an alcoholic. I wanted to leave, but didn't know how. Just as with my mother, my husband began beating me up after his drinking binges. My mother and I weren't talking. I had no idea where my father was and I didn't have any close friends. I felt resigned to my fate.

One night, with two black eyes and a bruised body, I got in my car and drove away. I ended up driving for several days until I came to a coastal town in Washington State. During the drive, I decided one thing—I would never trust a man again! I concluded that since my own father was abusive and violent and my husband turned out to be the same, then all men must be bad.

8

Eventually I got a job as a waitress and began to carve out a simple yet lonely life for myself. My mother and I began talking every week on the phone. It felt good to be in communication with her again.

One day, a customer brought in an ad for a workshop on relationships. "Well that's sure not for me!", I remarked with much sarcasm. "I never want to be with a man again. I've had it, I'm done."

That seemed like a strong statement for a twenty-five-year-old woman to be making, so she teased me a little, then seriously urged me to go. "You are too young to give up on relationships," she said with a smile. She then ripped out the ad and placed it in my pocket.

Returning to my lonely room in the boarding house, I looked at the ad. Something about the possibility of a loving relationship intrigued me. Then all my fears came up and I ripped up the ad and threw the pieces in the garbage.

When I went to bed that night, I felt lonelier than I had felt in years. Usually I was very good at holding in all my feelings, but that night I couldn't keep them down. I felt the pain of having an abusive father, then having the same experience repeated in my marriage. I felt lonely, but so fearful of ever trusting again. I hadn't given much attention to spiritual matters, yet on that lonely night I prayed to be able to trust again. After a while I slept peacefully.

When I awoke, I knew with certainty that I must go to the seminar on relationships. Something seemed to have happened to me during the night. Then I remembered my prayer. "Maybe this is the help I'm needing," I thought as I rummaged through the garbage to retrieve the ripped-up ad. Finding one piece with the phone number intact, I called and registered. I felt lighter and happier than I had felt since I was a young child.

The day of the seminar came and I felt a strange combination of fright and enthusiastic anticipation. I quietly entered the room and saw that it was filled with people. The frightened part of me grew and I almost ran out of the room, but the enthusiastic part of me found my way to a quiet corner where I awaited directions.

Right off the bat, a young man came over to sit next to me. He said he felt a little overwhelmed by all the people and needed to find a friend. He told me a joke and made me laugh. Something about his manner made me relax. I found myself opening to him. He told me he was part American Indian and his name was Sun Bear. Sun Bear and I spent the entire seminar together. At the end he asked for my phone number and I gladly gave it to him. We began dating. When Thanksgiving came, I asked if he would come to my mother's house with me for the weekend. He agreed.

My mother greeted us both with warm hugs. She began to ask Sun Bear about his past. I was getting annoyed with my mother for probing into Sun Bear's life so deeply. Finally she stopped and a very strange expression crossed her face. Abruptly she excused herself and was gone a long time. I apologized to Sun Bear for my mother's unusual behavior.

Finally, she came back, holding a photo album. "Sun Bear," she asked with choking emotion, "Did you have a different name in childhood?"

He looked uncomfortable with this question and I was seriously annoyed, then he responded, "Yes, my mother and friends called me Bobby."

My heart began to pound wildly. With that my mother pulled out a picture of two little children on a swing. "I believe this is you, Sun Bear, with my daughter Jennifer."

Love had guided us back together after seventeen lonely years. We have now been married for thirty years and feel so grateful to be together again. And oh—I still love to listen to his jokes.

℘ Jennifer Walker

The Mystery Man from Hartwick

• • • • • • • •

FOR AS LONG as I can remember, I have always wanted to be a doctor. Perhaps my desire was inspired by the tall kindly pediatrician, Dr. Schmidt, who came to our home when I was very sick with the measles. Perhaps it was simply an innate knowledge.

Like many people, I found the deepest peace in solitude. I considered myself lucky to move from Brooklyn at the age of six and spend the rest of my childhood growing up at the edge of a neighborhood in Elmsford, New York, in a house bordering a vast area of farmland and woods. I loved playing with the kids in the neighborhood, but most of all I loved wandering the open spaces for hours by myself, making up stories about being a pioneer doctor.

At the age of eighteen, in my senior year at Sleepy Hollow High School in Tarrytown in 1964, I finally started noticing girls, especially one particular girl. I went out with Becky for three months. Although it was puppy love, it was still my heart's first awakening, my first time kissing a girl and holding hands in public proclaiming to the world that I was now in a relationship.

At the same time, I was waiting to hear back from the colleges to which I had applied. Although I was a fairly good student, especially when a subject interested me (or a teacher made the subject interesting), the process of applying to colleges felt unimportant to me. In fact, and this is embarrassing for me to admit, I had so little motivation that my mother ended up doing most of the work for me, researching schools and filling out applications.

Then, almost as suddenly as my brief relationship began, Becky announced she didn't want to see me anymore. I didn't get it. A week later I saw her in school walking down the hall hand-in-hand with another boy. That sight really drove home the fact that the relationship was over. Up to that point I held out the hope that she didn't really mean what she had said.

I was heartsick. I remember lying in bed with an awful empty feeling inside and wished good old Dr. Schmidt had a remedy for my heartache. It was even worse than the time I was cut from the baseball team, even though the other players said I was just as good as they were. I felt discriminated against, being the only Jew trying out for a team of mostly Catholic Italians, who were clearly favored by the Italian coach. The pain and rejection was enormous. Baseball was my passion. When I wasn't wandering the woods and fields by myself, I was organizing a baseball game with as many kids as I could round up from the neighborhood. But the pain of being rejected by Becky was even worse.

To make matters worse, one after another rejection letters started to come in from prospective colleges. It didn't seem to make any difference to me—I already felt hopelessly rejected. Then came the rejection letter from the last college, my safety choice, the one I felt surely would accept me.

It was the final blow. My dreams of becoming a doctor seemed far away now. Yes, I hadn't made the baseball team, but I survived that. I could still play baseball. Yes, I lost my girlfriend but I could survive that too. Somewhere deep within me I knew there was someone somewhere waiting for me. I had gotten a taste of love, a feeling of connection with another. It had awakened in me a deeper yearning to travel to even higher places of joy and love, to experience that wonderful feeling of being at home with another.

But now all these college rejections. It was just too much for me to take. It wasn't even that I wanted to go to these particular colleges. It was more the picture I had in my mind that I would be a pre-medical major in college that next fall. It was so confusing to have such a clear picture inwardly that didn't match what was happening on the outside.

I became depressed. While my friends were whooping and congratulating each other on their acceptances, I was forlornly wandering the school halls, head hung low, still trying to avoid seeing Becky and her new boyfriend.

It was precisely at one of these moments, while trudging in a fog of self-pity from one class to another, that a voice over the loudspeaker crackled me to attention.

"Barry Vissell," said the school secretary's voice, "Please report to the principal's office."

My immediate reaction was one of fear. I had a mischievous side to me that sometimes got me into trouble. What had I recently done that might have caused a call to the principal's office? My mind went wild surveying the list of possibilities, the pranks that might have been discovered.

Entering the secretary's office, I felt immensely relieved to see her smile. Whew, I thought to myself, I'm not in trouble. She ushered me to an inner office, where I was welcomed by a neatly dressed, smiling man who appeared to be in his thirties. He shook my hand and said he was from Hartwick College in Oneonta, New York. He took probably one minute to tell me about the school, and then pointed to some papers on the table next to him.

"This is an application for admission to Hartwick College. With the help of your school officials, we've filled it out with information from your school records."

I was beginning to feel dizzy. Had I been watching too many episodes of *The Twilight Zone?* I had never heard of Hartwick College. Was this some kind of joke to get even with me for all the pranks I had played on others? First my mother did most of the work applying to colleges that ended up rejecting me. Now this strange guy was filling out another application to a college I've never heard of.

But I didn't have much time to ponder these things. Quickly the man pulled a shiny pen out of his sportcoat pocket and extended it to me. "If you'd like to join us next fall at Hartwick, sign here," he said placing a finger of his other hand next to a line at the bottom of the application.

Suddenly I didn't know what to do. "Can I have some time to think about this?" I stammered. "It seems like such an important decision."

"Sure, sure," he confidently answered, "Take a few minutes."

I had hoped he would have offered me a few days.

I paused probably fifteen seconds, solemnly took the pen from him and proceeded to sign away four years of my life. He retrieved his pen and thanked me with an almost uncomfortably warm yet genuine smile. His final words as he walked me out of the office still ring in my ears: "I promise you. You'll never regret this decision."

"How does he know?" was my thought.

But somehow I felt at peace. Driving home on my old Vespa motorscooter, I felt a joy and lightness bubbling up from within me, feelings I had almost forgotten about. It felt like my old Vespa had wings. Upon arriving home, I remember the incredulous look in my mother's face as I triumphantly announced, "Mom, I'm going to Hartwick College next fall."

It's funny about youth. I gave no real thought to who that man was, or how he found out about me. I just accepted it as a matter of course and showed up that next fall at Hartwick College in the rolling Catskill Mountains of upstate New York.

I saw Joyce for the first time at a soccer game later that fall. I was sitting on the bleachers with some dorm buddies. We were acting "cool," in other words, more grown-up and sophisticated than we really were. I was in college now, and I wanted to show everyone that I was an adult.

Suddenly there was a loud outburst of almost hysterical laughter a few rows above me. I turned to see who could be making such an immature display of emotion. It was an attractive female freshman with large green captivating eyes. She was doubled up with laughter with a group of her friends. How childish, I thought, but I couldn't take my eyes off her. How uncool, I judged, but my heart felt powerfully drawn to her. I forced myself to look back at the soccer game but my curiosity overwhelmed me. I looked back. Who was this girl who cared so little about being cool? She was simply allowing herself to have an outrageously good time. I, on the other hand, was caught in a world of social conformity, a world of playacting to get the approval of others. I felt shame, than embarrassment, and looked away again.

For the next several weeks, I tried to get the image of this girl out of my mind but I couldn't. But we didn't run into one another again.

Then I applied at the school cafeteria for a job as student-waiter to help with college expenses. The job paid a whole dollar an hour. For some reason, boys and girls were paired up to work as a team serving a row of tables. And who did I happen to be assigned with? You guessed it, Joyce. Soon I found myself laughing just as hard as she did. We had such a fun time serving the students at our tables, that it was contagious. It seemed like our row of tables had the loudest laughter in the cafeteria. In Joyce's presence, my heart blossomed, my soul and body loosened up, and most importantly in the ensuing months, I fell in love.

Now, as I look back, thirty-six years later, thirty-six years of living and loving together, I can see the divine guidance behind all these events—my failed relationship with Becky, the "angel" with the college application, the soccer game, the cafeteria job.

Recently, at one of our workshops, I told this story and someone pointed out, given the work we do, the appropriateness of the name, "Hartwick" College. Joyce and I never thought about this before. I got the image of a wick, like a candle wick. By itself, a wick cannot sustain a flame, but in the candle it has the ability to channel the fuel up through itself. A "heart-wick" is a conduit for the energies of the heart to burn ever more brightly, lighting up the world with "heart-light." And that's exactly how I feel about the love Joyce and I share.

Barry Vissell

The Voice of Guidance

I WAS BORN into a loving family of mother, father, and older brother. My mother had lost twin boys at birth two years earlier so I was regarded as a miracle by my parents. My birth was also celebrated by my seven aunts, who were like mothers to me, as well as my uncles and fourteen cousins, all of whom lived a short drive from our home. In other words, I was blessed by a large and loving family, surrounded constantly by people who doted on me and believed in me. And yet there was a undeniable sadness that could always be seen in my eyes. I have many pictures of family gatherings, which occurred whenever someone had a birthday, there was a holiday, or someone simply felt a need to gather. Amid pictures of all this joy and love, I always had a faraway look of sadness. Even with everything seemingly right, there was something missing.

One of my early childhood memories occurred at night in that state between sleeping and waking. I remember lying in my bed feeling as if I were in a prison. Seeking an exit, I directed my thoughts to each part of my body. "There must be a way out of here!" I desperately thought to myself. My four-year-old body felt heavy and foreign. I, on the other hand, felt light and totally separate from it. Getting out of the prison was the most important thing to me. Over and over again I raced throughout my body, in my mind looking for an escape.

Finally in total frustration I yelled, "Get me out of here, I want to be free again!" My father was at my side in an instant. He told me I was just having a bad dream and carefully brought me in bed to lie between him and my mother. I felt comforted, but not free. Gradually I returned to sleep. These occurrences happened until I was eighteen, although with less and less frequency.

At the same time, our pediatrician, Dr. Jacobson, was concerned with what he referred to as my "failure to bloom." My mother was doing her best to feed me well-balanced meals, yet

I had little interest in eating. I had plenty of friends, activities, and fun in my life. Yet when it came to nourishing my body with food, I had little desire.

Dr. Jacobson finally told my worried mother, "She hasn't quite decided if she wants to be here. I suggest you buy her a pet." A small dog named Nicky was bought, plus a cat and goldfish. The pets gave me great joy, yet they did not take from me this faraway sadness that kept me from nourishing my body and being truly happy.

When I was seven, the good doctor decided I needed a tonsillectomy. "This will help her to bloom," he told my mother with confidence. As much as I honor this man for his wisdom and compassion, this was not a good plan. The operation and overnight stay was the most traumatic experience of my young life. The tonsillectomy gave me a horrible sore throat that seemed to go on forever. The nighttime experiences of feeling trapped in my body and wanting to get out grew in intensity and frequency. I lost weight and, rather than blooming, faded a little bit more. The doctor told my mother to give the tonsillectomy a bit more time to work its magic.

One aspect of my family life that I did not like was my brother's teasing. My brother is a genius in intelligence and humor who could captivate an entire family gathering with his wit. I generally thought he was funny until he made me the object of his jokes. I was sensitive and my feelings were easily hurt. When my brother teased me, my eyes would fill with tears. My parents said I was too sensitive and couldn't take a joke. I was told to go to my room if I needed to cry. Once sent to my room, I would feel more lonely and hurt than ever.

His teasing grew in intensity and I continued to be sent to my room for my tears. "You can't be happy in your life until you learn to be less sensitive," my parents would say in exasperation. "Learn to take a joke!" My parents meant well and were sincerely seeking to help me learn how to brush off teasing remarks. However, being isolated was very painful to me.

During one of these times of being sent to my room, something happened that changed my life forever. I was nine years old. As usual I went to my bed and cried as a growing despair grew within me. Suddenly I felt myself enfolded by loving arms. No one was with me, yet I felt a strong loving presence speak to me in my heart, *"Someone is now growing up who you are meant to be with. This person will understand your feelings, will love your sensitivity, and will hold you when you cry. You will recognize him as a tall, dark-haired young man who will become a doctor."*

Through the energy of this loving guidance, I felt instantly connected to this person who was to come into my life. I did not doubt for an instant that what was spoken to me was true. I suddenly relaxed deeply for perhaps the first time in my young life. What had been missing had been promised to me. The sadness was no more.

I began to gain weight, my cheeks flushed with color and health. The doctor was convinced the tonsillectomy finally started to work. My life went on as usual with typical childhood joys and sorrows. My brother continued to tease me and I was still sent to my room for crying, but I never again felt totally alone. I felt connected to my tall, dark-haired special friend who would understand my tears and sensitivity. He was in the process of growing up too, and we would meet when the time was right.

This knowledge gave me untold peace, especially throughout adolescence. While my girlfriends dated and were asked out to proms, and my mom worried about my lack of social life, I was seldom concerned that I was seemingly alone. I had an ever-growing awareness of my connection to my future beloved. My first boyfriend was short, blond, and wanted to be a teacher. I enjoyed the thrills of holding hands, kissing, and going out on dates. When he suddenly dropped me for another girl, I was not hurt at all. I had never taken the relationship seriously. Obviously he was not the one.

Feeling the loving arms of the unseen being and hearing the still voice in my heart led me into a very spiritual life. I rose early in the morning to read inspirational books and to pray. My mother, who is a very spiritual person, was a constant source of reading material and inspiration to me. Half of my life seemed to be spent in church, going to services, Sunday school, youth groups, and choir. Though my mother was a Presbyterian, she wanted me to be open to great leaders of other faiths. Gandhi was one of her heroes and she exposed me to many of his teachings. This introduction to other spiritual views has profoundly affected my life. It also opened the door to meeting my beloved.

I had been a good student in high school, with high SAT scores. I could have gone to any college I wanted. Looking past the prestigious East Coast schools, I settled on Hartwick College. "Why Hartwick?", my peers wanted to know. No one had ever heard of it. But my minister's sister had gone to

Hartwick and described it as a small, Protestant college in the Catskill Mountains. Something clicked inside me and it was the only school I applied to. It was one of those decisions that felt right, but had no rational explanation.

In the fall of 1964, I arrived at Hartwick College to begin my freshman year. Though I missed my parents and family very much, I felt a joy almost bursting inside of me. I was so happy I literally skipped wherever I went and shouted greetings of hello or have a nice day to everyone I passed. My enthusiasm was so great I began to be criticized for it. People thought I was faking it or just putting on a show. I consciously tried to tone down my joy. Sometimes I would question myself with, "Why are you so happy? People think you're weird. Why are you behaving this way?" I didn't know why. I just knew that I'd wake up filled with mounting excitement.

I worked as a waitress in the college cafeteria to earn my spending money. The waiter assigned to work with me was a tall dark-haired boy. I didn't take much interest in him. He was very skinny, shy, and looked so boyish. At the end of our shift we were cleaning the tables together when, to be polite, I asked him his name.

"Barry," he said with almost too big of a smile.

"Do you have a major?" I asked.

"Pre-med," was his casual reply.

In that moment a shiver ran through my body. I looked at him more intently. Not my type, I decided, looking at his boyish face and weird way of dressing.

Several days later when I saw him at a snowball fight between the boys' and girls' dorms, a similar shiver ran through my body. The next week we went out on a date and, walking back to the dorm in the snow, we held hands and kissed good night. What a kiss—my life would never be the same. We were too young and immature to understand the powerful energy that passed between us. I simply thought "Boy, he really knows how to kiss!"

It was like the kiss upon Snow White's lips causing her eyes to open. In that kiss was the deepest feeling of connection and of coming home. Suddenly I knew why I had been so excited for the three months I had been at college. I had sensed his closeness.

Shortly after meeting Barry, I had one more experience of lying in bed and feeling like I was trapped inside my body. I hadn't had this experience in many years and was surprised by the return of this childhood experience. As I was trying to get out of my body, I again heard the same gentle, guiding voice of my childhood say, *"Now you can feel at home here and do not need to leave again."* I had found the tall dark-haired doctor-to-be who would love and care for me so deeply.

❦ Joyce Vissell

What's in a Name?
. . . .

FOR AS LONG as I can remember, I have seemed to know the name of the woman with whom I would spend my life. It was supposed to be Amanda. I really don't know how I knew this; I don't consider myself psychic. I do vaguely remember a few dreams in my adolescence including that name, and then one more in my mid-twenties. But more than the dreams, I have always seemed to possess the knowledge that her name would be Amanda.

On my thirtieth birthday, I looked back at my life with sadness. I had met several Amandas, but none were right for me. I tried very hard to be with one of these women, to make her somehow fit as a lover, but it didn't work. It ended painfully. I had other relationships with women of different names. These, too, were painful as I tried to fight against my inner knowing, or even to pretend that I didn't have this bit of information locked in my heart.

I also felt anger. It felt like a handicap to have such a precise qualification for my life partner. I felt limited in my relationships. My friends could enjoy the simple pleasure of dating with an open mind and heart. I felt biased, at times even cursed.

For example, there was a beautiful young woman, Heather, who lived in the apartment next door to mine. I felt attracted to her. I felt comfortable with her. When she greeted me with that warm smile of hers, I felt her genuine caring. If her name was Amanda, I would have leapt for joy. But I had to hide my feelings for fear of breaking her heart—and mine.

One Saturday morning, I decided to take a walk. My apartment building bordered a large park with tree-lined walkways. As I stepped out into the hall, I noticed Heather was also leaving her apartment. We said hello—why did she have to disarm me so completely with her smile? Walking together toward the stairs, I told her I was going for a walk in the park.

She said, "I was heading that way too. Would you mind if I came along?"

"No, I'd like that," I quickly replied.

Then came that old familiar conflict. Enthusiasm to be with someone I really liked, and fear of getting involved with someone I would end up leaving.

For the walk, however, I managed to put aside my worries. Being in Heather's presence was so comfortable, so familiar. We had a great time, with much laughter as well as some serious conversation about our lives.

Later, alone in my apartment, I started to panic. One walk in a park and I was falling in love. How could this be? I again felt angry at my "curse," and resolved that I needed to follow my own path, to choose the person with whom I would spend time. I refused to be controlled by a name anymore. I would spend as much time as I wanted with Heather. And I certainly wanted to spend more time with her.

I knocked on Heather's door later that afternoon. It was almost like she expected me, and warmly invited me in. She showed me her apartment. We talked for hours; it was amazing how much we had in common. We talked about our spirituality. Although we came from seemingly diverse backgrounds, we shared the same basic beliefs about a Higher Power that was as much a part of us as it was a part of everything in the universe.

It was obvious that we liked each other wholeheartedly. I told her how comfortable I felt in her presence. Her smile told me she felt the same. I knew I needed to tell her about "the Amanda thing" but, before I could begin, she started talking about her childhood.

"Tyler," she began, "I didn't have an easy childhood. I can't remember any time my parents sincerely listened to me. You're such a good listener. I feel important in your presence."

"That's easy," I interrupted, "I can't remember ever enjoying listening to someone else this much."

Heather smiled, thanking me, then continued in more serious tones, "I felt pressured by my parents to live my life according to their beliefs, to follow in their footsteps. When I finished high school, I couldn't take it anymore. I chose a college as far away from home as possible. In my attempt to find myself and my own values, I did some wild living with partying, drugs, and sex. I even changed my name. . . ."

A bolt of electricity shot through me. "Heather," I interrupted again, almost afraid to ask, "what was your original name?"

She looked sad, then continued, "I hated my name. It has always been a reminder of an oppressed, controlled child I've been trying to run away from. But lately I've been feeling differently about that name. I'm considering going back to it, sort of reclaiming my lost childhood. What do you think of me going back to my childhood name, Amanda?"

"YES!!" I almost shouted. "I love the name Amanda!"

I could scarcely contain my excitement. My story tumbled out of my mouth. Her face went from puzzled, to amazed, then to excited. With tears in my eyes, I reached out and hugged Heather. No—Amanda!

That was nine years ago. Amanda now loves her name. Our son and daughter like to call her Amanda.

© Tyler San Marcos

Heart of Love
. . . .

MY BROTHER, DANNY, was born ten minutes before me. Inseparable from the beginning, we could only sleep if the other was close by. If one woke up, the other was soon to follow. Our two younger siblings were born within four years of our birth. Our parents were so busy with them that Danny and I took care of each other. If someone asked us what our names were, we would say in unison, "Danny"—or maybe the next day we would say, "Darlene." As far as we were concerned, we were one and the same.

Throughout elementary school, junior and senior high, we ate every lunch together. The friends we had were always "our" friends. When we chose the same college, our father finally put his foot down and would not allow us to room together. We were assigned separate rooms with roommates of the same sex. I guess our parents hoped we would begin to operate more as individuals, but Danny and I continued to spend as much time together as possible. We began dating, but always as double dates. The truth is, we both knew we couldn't spend the rest of our lives together, as we both wanted to have families of our own, but we were also so fulfilled in each other's presence. Danny was my brother, my best friend, my main support, my confidant, and the funniest person I knew.

Although I liked doing everything with Danny, the pastime I enjoyed the most was painting. Danny was a sensitive, trained artist, who drew heavenly landscapes, with pictures of angels and little children. He could draw the most beautiful faces. His weakness, or so he said, was painting hands. In contrast, my strength was painting hands in their infinitely different positions. Often, Danny would ask me to paint hands on the angels or children in his paintings. When Danny and I were painting together, we felt exceptionally close to each other and also to our Creator.

One evening, we stayed very late finishing our work in the art classroom. Driving home, there was a special feeling between us. Suddenly, there was a car in our lane coming straight toward us. We were hit before I could even scream.

The driver of the other car was a teenager who had had too much to drink at a party. He was killed instantly. Danny was seriously hurt and rushed to the hospital. I was shaken, but not badly hurt. I rode in the ambulance with Danny. The doctors were grave and honest, Danny had sustained irreparable brain damage. There wasn't anything that could be done. As his only relative present at the time, a surgeon approached me about the possibility of donating his heart for transplant. I got my parents on the phone and we all agreed to donate Danny's heart so someone else might live. As Danny lay in a coma, his heart was removed and rushed to a waiting donor.

The two years that followed were black years for me. I attempted suicide three times, was hospitalized and given drugs I refused to take. I did not know how to live without my beloved Danny. My parents and friends tried, to no avail, to get me interested in life again.

A friend finally got through and convinced me one day to go to a local art show with her. I was trying to enjoy looking at the art, mostly for my friend, when suddenly I stopped in my tracks. There were paintings that were so similar to Danny's I could hardly believe it. I looked closely at the name just to be sure. I was told the artist would return in an hour. I waited, just mesmerized by the artwork. An hour later, a young man approached me and introduced himself as John. I felt a strange affinity to him. We talked for the rest of the day about art, then I gave him my phone number and went home.

Back at my apartment, I could think of nothing else but John. I wanted to see him again more than anything else. I was angry at myself for not getting his phone number. Two agonizing weeks went by before he finally called me. We made a date to walk in the park. I could not understand my feelings, but I felt as if I had already fallen in love with him. I felt happy for the first time since Danny's death.

At the park, John and I walked and talked and it felt as if time stood still. I told him about Danny and my suffering of the past two years. John reached out and held me and, for the first time since Danny died, I felt comforted. While my tears flowed, I felt Danny's arms around me as well as John's, and I felt at home. I knew in that moment that I wanted to spend the rest of my life with John. He shared that he had never felt such love for another person as he did for me.

John and I spent as much time as we could together. One morning, I asked John to tell me how he happened to begin painting. He shared the story of his life. He was born with a congenital heart disease. He had always dreamed of becoming an artist, but his health problem occupied much of his attention and energy. He told me of the years he was in and out of hospitals and finally he was in the hospital for what looked like the last time. He was dying of heart failure. His only hope was a heart transplant but the doctors gave very little hope of one coming his way in time.

One night, he was rushed to the operating room and quickly told that a heart was on its way. He woke the next day with a healthy heart pumping in his chest. The transplant was a success and he soon left the hospital to begin a new life. He immediately launched himself into his art. He hadn't stopped painting since his operation and concluded by saying, "Painting is my life's passion, Darlene. I feel the most connected to God when I paint."

I held my breath while he spoke, my arms covered with goosebumps. I asked in a slow whisper, "Was your operation in March two years ago?"

"Yes!" was his stunned response as we both were realizing the possibility of what had happened. We held each other for a long while, not daring to speak as the growing truth was emerging.

Finally I spoke, "John, I never wanted to know who Danny's heart recipient was. We only learned that it was a success."

Soon after, I placed a call to the hospital and asked them to research who received my brother's heart. While we waited for the research, we studied John's paintings together. The faces on the people were beautiful. It was only then that I noticed and pointed out how he concealed hands behind objects. "I have trouble painting hands, so I put them behind flowers or animals or other people," John remarked.

The phone rang and we held each other as I received the

information from the hospital that I already knew. Danny's heart was successfully transplanted to John Yager.

John and I were married and, in a beautiful and sacred way, Danny's love is with us every moment.

⊛ *Darlene Yager*

Finding My Life Partner
. . . .

IT WAS THE spring of 1989. I was thirty-three years old, single, living in Colorado, and wondering if I would ever find my life partner. The latter part of my teens and the better part of my twenties had been spent in three somewhat long-term relationships, the first of which had lasted over six years.

The last five years had been devoted primarily to spiritual pursuits. It had been the first time in my adult life that I had no partner, affording me the opportunity to deepen my yoga and meditation practice, travel around the world, and follow whatever creative pursuit inspired me at any given moment. Most importantly, it allowed me to spend some quiet time on my own. I look back on that time with great reverence, for I really got to know myself as a friend.

Throughout this time, however, the deepest part of my heart kept calling out for its mate. I felt content, but not complete. I even explored the world of casual dating for the first time in my life. It was entertaining, but empty.

I developed the following affirmation to express my heart's desire:

31

"By the irresistible power of divine magnetism, I now draw to myself the wonderful romance, right marriage, and happy home with my true soul companion, who is mine by divine right, and who now manifests in my life, under grace, in the perfect way."

I wrote this affirmation over and over in my journal. I sang it and meditated upon it, until my being was imbued by it. It was ever on my lips and in my heart. My life continued joyfully, yet underneath it all my heart was lonely, calling for its partner.

In early summer, I visited some friends who live on an organic farm in Colorado. In their home I found a copy of Joyce and Barry Vissell's book, *The Shared Heart.* I remember being very drawn to the cover of the book, the title, and the concept. I began reading it and could not put it down. As I was leaving, my friend gave me the book, which I shudder to admit I continued to read while driving back home. After finishing *The Shared Heart,* I read their next book, *Models of Love.* I felt drawn to Barry and Joyce and inspired by their relationship. I put my name on their mailing list; I knew that I wanted to meet them.

In late summer I ended a three-month relationship. The man that I had been seeing was a great guy, but I felt no deep soul connection with him. I awoke one morning feeling suffocated, and realized in that one poignant moment that I would rather be single for the rest of my life than be in a relationship with the wrong person. This was a very liberating moment for me. I felt that I was destined to be in a committed relationship and to be a mother, and yet I finally felt truly at peace and surrendered to God's will. I prayed to be shown how to serve God in the highest way.

Fall is a glorious time to be in the Colorado mountains. The last weekend of September was a few short days away and I wanted to spend it backpacking, immersed in the changing colors of the Aspen trees, but none of my friends were free to join me except for the man with whom I had recently broken up.

I had received Joyce and Barry's fall newsletter, which I had promptly "filed" in my stack of junk mail. Even though the newsletter was in a place where I seldom look, I kept feeling drawn to it. On Monday morning in the last week of September, as I sat in my office looking out at the mountains, I finally picked up the newsletter. I was instantly drawn to a workshop they were leading that upcoming weekend in the Santa Cruz mountains entitled "Finding Your Life Partner." A rather bold title, I remember thinking. I wanted to go, and yet it seemed impractical to travel to California for a weekend. After all, I really did want to backpack that weekend. But my inner voice kept chanting the mantra "you should go, you should go!" The more I attempted to ignore it and focus on my work, the more incessant it became: "You Should Go, YOU SHOULD GO!"

Finally, two days before the weekend I decided to call and see if there was space in the workshop. There was. Then I telephoned the airlines and discovered that given such short notice the flight would be too expensive. Once again the newsletter was returned to my stack of junk mail. Then from the depths of my being an almost comical directive arose: "try 'mileage plus,' try 'mileage plus'!"

"This is ridiculous," I remember thinking. I had no idea how many miles I had. I hadn't even received a statement in months. As it turned out, I had just enough miles for a ticket, provided I would pay a $25 Fed Ex fee, as by then I would be departing in less than forty-eight hours! Once again, I sat in my office, looking out at the mountains. It was another pivotal moment. I mused, "Do I want to spend the weekend in a beautiful place with the wrong person, or do I want to spend the weekend in another beautiful place, meet Barry and Joyce, and move forward by affirming what I really wanted to create in my life?" I dropped my backpacking plans.

That night, as I lay in bed reading about the workshop in the newsletter, I noticed that a man named John Astin would be providing the music. His name sounded vaguely familiar, and I began to wonder if he was the same man that I had met at a Yogananda meditation retreat years before. This man had sung so beautifully, and I had purchased a cassette tape from him. My car stereo had destroyed all of my tapes except that particular one. So I just kept this one tape in my deck and played it over and over again for the past three years. I knew all the songs by heart, but was not sure of the name of the singer. I was curious, so I crawled out of my warm bed, crept down to my cold car, and checked the tape. Sure enough, it was John's tape. I remembered him as having long hair, a beard, and thick glasses. Other than his music I had felt no attraction to him in the brief moments that we had met.

When I arrived for the weekend, I was looking forward to a special time of quiet retreat. I arrived early, set up my tent in the redwoods, went for a run, and then wandered down to the kitchen for a cup of tea. As I came through the door I saw a man talking to the cook. Although the long hair, beard, and glasses were gone, I knew in an instant that it was John. We took one look at each other and I knew inside that my life would never be the same. It was as if time stood still as we glimpsed deeply into one another's soul. It felt like a reunion, as if we already deeply knew each other. That weekend we spent virtually every moment together, and although John didn't fit my "checklist" of who I thought I wanted for my life partner, he inspired me to dwell in God more than anyone else ever had. It soon became very clear to me that I wanted to be with him forever.

We talked three or four times a day after that weekend and visited twice during the month of October. On my thirty-fourth birthday, one month after we met, John asked me to marry him. Eight months later Joyce and Barry married us in Colorado. Five years later we gave birth to our little girl, Erin, who is now four years old.

I'm so glad that I waited for my heart to say "YES!" one hundred percent.

⊛ Kat Trueblood-Astin

The Concert That Changed My Life

• • • • • • •

TIME FOR FUN was low on my list. I was extremely busy with a full-time college course load, coupled with a thirty-hour work week. So when my mother called to invite me to a concert, of course I said no. Then, while leaving church the following Sunday morning, as I was climbing the stairs I was pulled back down by a strong feeling. At the bottom of the stairs, I found an enticing poster which had caught my eye on the way out. To my surprise, it advertised the concert my mother had spoken of a few days earlier. The electrifying response I had to this poster was so distinct that I soon called my mother to confirm that I would attend the concert.

The performer was Karl Anthony and he gave a performance that was unlike anything I had experienced before. I laughed, I cried, and I sang. Before this moment I would only mouth the words to "Happy Birthday." Now I was in some kind of altered state of joy where it seemed anything was possible. Out of this excitement and joy came a thought that had never occurred to me in my twenty-five years: *If* I were to ever get married, it would be to a man like him!

I never pictured my life including marriage or children. My passion was travel and learning about other cultures. I had a deep desire to be involved in service work. I envisioned myself in the Peace Corps, or some similar organization, devoted to working in the dirt with people.

After the concert I waited in a long receiving line to speak a few words to Karl. When it was my turn he looked at me with gentle blue eyes, smiled, and gratefully took in my words of praise. I was a bit nervous so I spoke for no more than thirty seconds, enjoyed a brief hug, and left. I proceeded to my night job at a shelter for battered women and children.

I thought about that concert for weeks. With each new thought came a flicker of reevaluation of my life. I realized that

I was putting so much time into work and school that my close relationships were suffering.

As a result of that concert, I decided to let go of two jobs and keep one. I also quit a thirteen-year habit of smoking two packs a day. For days after the concert I was still deeply affected, so I sent Karl a note. At the concert he'd mentioned not feeling well. I found myself concerned for his well-being. It was obvious he gave generously, so I encouraged him to take care of himself and I included a rose quartz crystal, which was to act as a reminder. I had some hesitation to send the note, fearing I would appear to be a groupie. In the end, I decided it was a small gesture of appreciation for all he had given, and was the least I could do. He wrote back, telling me the crystal was under his pillow along with his dreams.

A year passed. The flickering thought of marriage faded as easily as it had come, yet I was still benefiting from having given up cigarettes and changing my lifestyle. I gave more to my relationships with others and found myself less fatigued over work.

It was Mother's Day and my mother wanted to start her special day with the family attending church. After the service, we were all eager to go to breakfast, but my mother wanted to socialize and, since it was her day, the rest of us patiently waited. While waiting, I just happened to glance at the event board and saw that Karl Anthony was again coming to the area the very next weekend—only the venue of his performance was almost two hours away. I became very excited to reconnect with the magical feeling his performance inspired the year before. As I thought about the logistics, however, I became disappointed.

It was too far away and would just take too much time for my busy schedule. After further thought, I decided I would make the trip to talk with him about getting involved in the peace movement. Justifying it as a career-development trip somehow gave it more value.

During the week between Mother's Day and the concert, some profound experiences occurred to assure my attendance at Karl's concert. I was working as a house parent for homeless teens in an alternative living program. I worked a seventy-two-hour weekend shift offering supervision, support, and life skills training to five teenage girls. One particular night of this weekend was typical with its adolescent ups and downs. Eventually the girls were safely tucked into bed and I soon followed.

In the middle of the night, I was abruptly awakened by an enormous flash of light. When the light subsided, a man stood at the foot of my bed. My throat and stomach tightened. My first thought was that an intruder was in the house. Recently there had been a drive-by shooting in the neighborhood. I quickly closed my eyes and pretended to be asleep, believing that if he didn't know I had seen him, maybe he would only rob the house and leave without hurting anyone. I kept as still as I possibly could, but I could feel my heart pound loudly in my chest. Petrified, I kept my eyes closed until I hoped to hear him leave, only I never heard anything. Then a very strange thing happened. I fell asleep.

The next morning, I awoke, surprised to be alive. I searched for evidence of a forced entry into the house. There was none. I checked on the girls. They were fine and had heard nothing. I was puzzled by this experience. The man I saw was as real as you and me. I was sure I hadn't been dreaming. Why was there no evidence of him being there?

I questioned the girls. Had they given out the house key to anyone? They assured me they hadn't. The very next night, I was again awakened by the same enormous flash of light and the same man stood at the foot of my bed. In spite of my apprehension, this time I had the courage to keep my eyes slightly opened. The man appeared to be young, dressed in tight, faded jeans and had the presence of a strong Native American warrior. His long blond hair glistened like a halo. We exchanged no words, but I found myself captured by the combination of his gentleness and confident masculinity. For ten minutes I watched him. He didn't move. He stood with his arms crossed out in front of him and stared at a picture of a young woman in the city which hung above the bed.

I gradually realized he was not an intruder, but a vision. I wanted to ask him questions but my throat was too tight with fear, though his presence was calm and nonthreatening. The glow from his hair was hypnotic and eventually drew me into a deep sleep.

Upon wakeful reflection, I knew this unexplainable experience was some type of spiritual messenger. I was actually a little upset with myself for not having the courage to speak up and ask this messenger why he appeared to me.

Sometime later, I realized this spiritual visitor embodied the same energy as Karl Anthony. "How ironic," I said to myself. "He is coming to town in a few days."

After this experience, I was more committed than ever to attend the concert. And what a surprise awaited me! Not only did Karl remember me, but he chose me to be on stage for the closing song and asked me out to dinner.

Karl and I had a great time at dinner, talking in a non-flirtatious way. The person I drove home with thought Karl was romantically interested in me, but I disagreed. Since I was not looking for a relationship, I was not sensitive to these kind of signals. I had been very hurt by a relationship three years prior and, at that turning point, had decided to put time into building a future for myself, developing a strong relationship with God, and to wait until I met a man of outstanding quality. I chose to focus on making a contribution to humankind, rather than a contribution to man. Yet Karl's soothing and nourishing qualities had begun to wiggle their way into my heart.

I soon received a call from Karl. He invited me to a conference in Colorado where he was presenting and where I could network with people about the peace movement. I was interested but was ambivalent because I would have to rearrange many recent commitments, and spend money I had worked hard to save. I thought a lot about it. Karl called me almost every day and asked about the likelihood of my attendance! The consistency of his action caught my attention. It was refreshing. I was used to men speaking more sweetly than their actions ever reflected.

Because it just felt right, I decided to do something out of character. I made all the necessary calls, took the risk of losing a new job, and missed the first week of summer school. I also took the chance of looking foolish by flying such a long distance to be with a long-haired musician from California who might not be as interested in me as I was in him.

Karl and I met at the airport. I arrived before him, so I greeted him at the gate. Moments before he walked off the plane, the freedom and empowerment I had felt in following my intuition turned to cold panic and fear of humiliation. "What am I doing here!" I inwardly screamed.

Fortunately Karl greeted me with a huge, warm smile and quickly offered to carry my luggage. During the hour and a half drive to the conference, Karl proceeded to tell me his life story. It was his way of dealing with nervous energy and laying it all out on the line, so as not to waste either of our time. As a therapist in training, I found my position of listener to be very comfortable. It was a beautiful moment in time, Karl allowing himself to be vulnerable and real.

That night we kissed under the full moon by a cool lake in the crisp mountain air. The next day we came to discover the beautiful lake where we kissed under the full moon was part of the camp's sewage treatment plant! The only thing Karl and I noticed that night was each other.

Karl and I had much in common and talked with ease for hours, actually for the entire weekend! We mountain biked, played volleyball, laughed, and ate together. I did none of the networking I originally planned to do. It soon became clear that Karl was exactly who I needed to be networking with. The magical weekend ended with Karl dedicating a song, "I Want To Be Your All," to me at the closing celebration of the retreat. I went home feeling extremely special, filled with gratitude for taking the risk.

We dated long distance for a year, meeting once a month in various states and talking daily on the phone. Some people voiced negative opinions about long-distance relationships. For us, long-distance dating was perfect. It allowed us to build a foundation of strong friendship. I learned that emotional closeness has nothing to do with proximity.

The second year, I moved out to California. I carved out a life of new friends, new interest, and a career. Karl toured much of the time. I enjoyed his thrill of performance and found it easy to support him and his dreams. The tours gave me plenty of time to find my own spotlight and to write my first book .

A year later, Karl unexpectedly proposed to me on my birthday, sixty feet in the air, on a high ropes course in upstate New York. Surrounded by a lush green forest, blue sky, and crisp mountain air, Karl kneeled on the platform and asked, "Will you live your life with me and be my bride forever?" Playing softly in the background was a love song Karl had written entitled "Jeanne." I was so filled with surprise and joy that I flew across the chasm between us into his arms and exploded with a glorious, "YES!"

                               ℗ *Jeanne Anthony*

Dakota

. . . .

I MOVED TO Seattle by default. I was hitching a ride with a friend and eventually heading to San Francisco. In the meantime, Seattle seemed like a fine place. I got a job at a local hospital, made some friends, and started really liking the Emerald City.

One day, when I had worked at the hospital for several

months, I had a vision of a little child asking me for acceptance as I walked to the bus stop after work. I wasn't sure if it was a boy or a girl. As this kind of thing was not an everyday occurrence for me, I chose to ignore it. But that wasn't easy. In the subsequent weeks I "saw" the child several more times.

At the hospital, I had met lots of people including a man named Hawk. One afternoon, as Hawk was doing some work on my computer, another coworker returned a copy of my first manuscript of poetry I had lent her. When she handed the manuscript to me, I felt a great power turn me toward Hawk and hand my work to him. I said, "Please read this." He looked surprised, said it often took him a long time to read things, and went on his way.

Hawk returned to my desk first thing the next morning with my manuscript in hand and a cassette tape for me. He told me he had been writing music for twenty years, but he hadn't seen the words to his music till he read my poetry. As I listened to his music on my Walkman that day, I had the haunting feeling that I knew this music.

As the weeks passed, we spent more and more time together, and felt our souls connect in love. My visions of the child asking for acceptance got stronger and stronger. It was always the same familiar voice asking acceptance. Acceptance of what? I wondered.

Finally, a dream revealed it to me. The child's name was Dakota. Dakota had picked Hawk and I for parents, and now wanted to know if we were going to accept.

Needless to say, when I told Hawk this story, he was surprised and shocked. He had two teenage children from a previous marriage. It took him two weeks to be able to discuss my dream with me.

We finally committed ourselves to each other and I started trying to get pregnant. We tried for a year. Nothing. There were questions as to whether or not I could even get pregnant. After lots of disappointing negatives on lots of pregnancy tests, Hawk and I decided to spend Christmas in celebration of our abundance instead of thinking about disappointment. He asked me to marry him that night. I wanted to be married to him. I wanted family and friends to know out loud and in public that I was in this forever.

We were married in June 1997 on the Summer Solstice and I got pregnant on our honeymoon! Apparently, this child knew that I had to completely surrender to love in order to make our lives work. We are now expecting our baby boy and are in awe of the abundance to which we have been guided. Thank you, Dakota, for making yourself so clearly known to your father and me. Thank you for helping to bring us together. And thank you for joining two art forms, music and poetry, as a gift to the world.

@ *Kara L. C. Jones*

My Vow
. . . .

I WAS A CHILD of sixteen when I met Josh. He was my first love. We were engaged when I was nineteen, married at twenty, and had our first child when I was twenty-one. Three years later our second child was born. Throughout our thirteen years of being together, we had many happy times as well as our share of the bumps and grinds of growing up and learning about being in a relationship. I found myself many times feeling like something was missing. I knew it wasn't lack of love, because I did love Josh and knew he loved me. Still I was aching for something more in our relationship, something spiritual.

My mother had given me the gift of a strong spiritual background. At nine years old, I began to meditate and connect to my own spirituality. As a teen, that part of me dropped off as "partying" with my friends moved to the forefront of my life. It was during that time that I came together with Josh. In my twenties, I resumed my spiritual quest but every time I began to search for my connection with spirituality, Josh and I would fight.

I remember a time when my mother had given me *A Course In Miracles* to study. Eagerly I began scanning the pages and excitedly shared my discoveries with Josh. Quickly my sharing escalated into a fight. The next day, sobbing, I threw the huge book into the garbage. Each time I tried to explore my spirituality, I turned away from it in order to have peace with Josh.

I tried to fill my spiritual void in other ways. I went to college and received my degree in psychology, went to counseling, and poured my heart and soul into raising my children. But still my heart ached deep inside.

Meanwhile, my older brother had just recently attended a couples workshop by Barry and Joyce Vissell. He had been so impressed with their work that he gave as a gift the Vissell's seven-day Hawaii retreat to his wife, our mom, and me. I was financially struggling at that time and never would have considered going had it not been a gift.

Once there, I found myself blossoming. I felt as if I was walking two feet above the ground with great joy in my heart. I thought, "I have come home," meaning home to myself.

I remember the first time I saw David. My mother and I walked into our shared retreat house and found a few people in the small kitchen downstairs talking. A trim man with wavy gray hair was sitting on the counter deeply engaged in conversation. My heart jumped. I immediately liked him. But I liked so many people there, so I thought nothing more of it.

The third night of the retreat, David and I, and a few other people, were in a group process together. I shared deeply about some of my pain in my marriage. He was kind and compassionate, and I felt safe and understood like no other time in my life. At the end of that night, I found myself alone with him on the lawn. He was telling me that he had been in many relationships and was ready now to find his life partner. As soon as he spoke those words, a voice inside of me yelled, "I'M YOUR LIFE PARTNER!"

"What?" I said to myself, "Come on Tracy! Sure he's a beautiful man but forget it! You are married and have two children!" In the next instant I shook my head and dismissed this strong inner voice.

David and I were drawn to each other like magnets. We talked on a deeper level than I had ever talked with anyone. But I was beginning to feel uncomfortable. Here I was connecting so deeply with this man while my husband and children were waiting at home for me! I told myself that I would never see David again and I would carry what he had given me into my relationship with Josh.

One day, I found myself walking alone on the grounds of the beautiful retreat center. I was reeling with joy from being connected with myself and my spirituality again. I stopped in my tracks and vowed to myself, "I will NEVER shut down my true self ever again!"

In the next instant, I knew Josh and I would never be able to make our relationship work. I knew that if I wanted to pursue my path, I couldn't be with Josh. This was a very scary and sad thought, so much so that I tried not to think about it.

As the retreat drew to a close, David and I knew we were getting close to the end of our time together. We found a special spot and sat facing each other, not touching, eyes open. As we looked into each other's eyes, we each had the most profound experience of our lives. We were able to see past our physical bodies, past our personalities, and straight into one another's souls. We became ecstatic as we saw the very essence of the other and at the same time our own essence reflected back. It was as if we were mirrors of each other's spirits. Then it seemed as if our souls rose out of our bodies and merged above our physical bodies.

This experience shook both of us to our core. Our connection had gone beyond personality into the mysterious place where souls meet.

Soon it was time to leave the retreat. Our hearts ached with the thoughts that we would never be together. But we accepted that fact.

My family and I stayed a few more days in Hawaii, visiting the volcano. The night before we were to leave, I emerged from the shower sobbing, expressing my deep fear of going home to Josh. My mother, brother, and sister-in-law held me trying to comfort me, telling me that it would all be okay. "But I've found something with David I don't think I'll ever have with Josh," I cried.

We flew home. Josh and the children picked me up at the airport. It felt strained with Josh. I felt he sensed something. Within the next few days I told him everything that had happened. Josh didn't understand and was deeply hurt. I found myself shutting down again, just like I had done all those past years. The pain and grief I felt in shutting myself down was so great that I cried and cried. I remembered my vow to myself in Hawaii but didn't know how I could keep it.

Two weeks later, I sat down to write a letter to David. I had to express how much I was missing him. As I was writing, the phone rang. I picked it up, somewhat annoyed that this special letter was being interrupted, "Hello?"

I could hardly believe what came next, "Hi Tracy, it's me, David."

My heart flooded with joy. Then there was a long silence.

Finally David tenderly said, "I knew you were feeling this way."

From that moment on we knew we couldn't stay away from each other. We began speaking to each other every day on the phone, writing letters, and seeing each other when we could.

Within two months, I made the decision to end my marriage with Josh and enter fully into relationship with David.

That was seven years ago. The first couple of years were rough, with my going through a very painful divorce, but we made it through. We married five and a half years after our meeting in Hawaii. During the rough times when we felt doubtful about the decisions we both made to come together, we would remind each other about the time in Hawaii when we felt divine guidance making it very clear to us that we were to be together.

The beauty, growth, and love David and I share is precious. I am ever thankful to God for leading me to share my life with him. And I have kept my vow to myself to freely embrace my spirituality.

⊛ Tracy Wikander

A Date To Remember

. . . .

IT WAS A lovely June Sunday in 1935. Our country was in a deep depression. My friend, Dorothy, and I planned to meet for a church program, after which we would walk to the Granada Theater. There we would enjoy a movie which cost just ten cents per person. That was about what we could afford on her salary of twelve dollars per week as a dental assistant and my salary of eight dollars a week as a secretary.

After the church meeting, we mingled a few minutes. A young man I slightly knew, Harlow, asked me to go downtown to the Shea's Buffalo Theater, where the cost was twenty-five cents per person.

I hesitated, saying, "I did make plans with my girlfriend."

The man persisted, "Hank Wollenberg wants to take you, but he asked me to invite you because he's too shy!"

Now I was startled! I had chosen to sit near Hank's mother and father for years at our church and I admired them a lot. My mother had died when I was six. I thought Mrs. Wollenberg was a beautiful mother and I liked to imagine that she was my own. I knew they had a son, but he was away at college and I never saw him. Hank had recently graduated and was living in Buffalo. Hank and Harlow had come to church that night looking for some girls to take to the movies.

Dorothy and I got together and decided this was too good an opportunity to pass up. The boys had Ford Coupes so we drove separately as couples. I do remember Dorothy saying, "I get the one with the better car! After all, I am older than you, Louise." As God would have it, Harlow had the better car.

Off we went in style to the theater. We sat in the balcony and rode down the long banister at the movie's end.

That evening turned out to be one of God's greatest gifts to both Dorothy and me. Dorothy and Harlow married and remained our very dear friends until their deaths.

Hank and I married in July 1939. The woman I had admired in church those many years ago, and who I had wished was my mother, became my mother-in-law. As I write this Hank and I are planning our sixtieth anniversary. We've had our ups and downs but with God planning our first meeting we have made even the downs into gifts.

℗ *Louise Wollenberg*

Editor's Note: Louise and Hank (Joyce's parents) celebrated their sixtieth anniversary in grand style. Seven weeks later, on August 19, 1999, Hank turned to his beloved wife and suggested they go out for dinner to celebrate again their wonderful marriage. "We have so much to be thankful for," he said, "let's go have a special time." The entire evening was so magical for them that people in the restaurant commented on their lovers' glow. They appreciated each other and their lives together. Twelve hours later, suddenly and unexpectedly, Hank died of a heart attack. He died with a smile on his lips, held in the arms of his beloved Louise and his granddaughters, Rami and Mira.

Revelation in the Shower

. . . .

ERIC AND I met in a twelve-step recovery group. He would call me, over a period of a couple of years, whenever he was feeling low. He was experiencing the raw hurt of the end of his marriage. My divorce had been especially difficult and I could offer him my empathy and understanding.

In June 1996, my mother had major abdominal surgery. I slept on her couch for three weeks. One day, after an especially hard night, I turned on the radio and heard Eric's voice. He was interviewing someone on a radio talk show. I was comforted by the kindness and intelligence in his voice. That evening, when my mother was settled, I called him to tell him he had been helpful to me.

Over the next few weeks, we went out to a couple of movies

and to see a friend's play. I didn't feel attracted to Eric as any-thing but a friend. I was even suspicious of his kind and patient attention.

I knew that my ex-husband Mark was to be married at the end of July. I had been preparing myself for the event for some time so that I could completely release him to his future happi-ness and at the same time free myself of any leftover resent-ment and pain.

About a week before Mark's wedding, Eric and I went to a movie. During a scary part of the movie, he reached out and put his hand on my leg. He then whispered, "Is my hand OK here?"

This small act of courtesy had a profound effect on me. As an incest survivor, I felt a seed of hopeful awareness being sown in my heart. Could it be possible to be touched by a man with respect? Might I have a voice in how and when I was touched?

Over the next several days I was flooded with memories during the day, and nightmares when I slept. The memories and dreams all had a common thread: my experience of hav-ing been wanted by men. All my life, men had been attracted to me and I had never really felt comfortable with their atten-tion. I prayed to be healed of my wounds in relation to men. Now I was having a new and refreshing insight. Being "wanted" could be a wondrous part of God's plan for me. I could be wanted in a healthy, loving way.

The actual day of Mark's wedding I spent in self-loving activity. I began with a long yoga class, then off to my twelve-step meeting, then a massage, a hike, and in the evening a meeting with my women's group. I had spoken to Eric the night before on Friday and we had made plans to get together Sunday night. By the time of the meeting with my women's group, I wasn't even thinking about Mark's wedding. I was excited to tell the women about my plans for Sunday night.

As Sunday rolled around, I was excited to see Eric. Then he dropped a bomb! He had begun a relationship with a woman across the country the month before, the first woman he had been intimate with since the end of his marriage. He told me he had already made plans to see her in a month or so.

I was shocked and confused, and thought to myself, "What's the deal God?" I felt like the butt of some cruel joke. What was the message and how had I misunderstood what had seemed to be such clear guidance? I was pulling toward Eric and now I found he was not fully available to me.

We had both separately promised ourselves that we would be honest with ourselves and with whomever we entered into a relationship. But this was not what I had in mind. I asked Eric right then if he would pray with me. I prayed a prayer that was both sincere and desperate: *"Help us see Your will in this."*

ERIC: I left Nancy's house that night full of conflicting feelings: sweetness and desire, love and fear, confusion and caring. We had spent an extraordinary five hours together. When Nancy asked if we could pray together part of my heart melted! This had never happened before with any woman, and I did not realize just how hungry I really was for a spiritual relationship.

I had a decision to make. I really liked Cynthia, who I had known since childhood. And I had no idea if I even had a future with Nancy. I went for a swim the next day, and the whole time my mind kept telling me how foolish I was, throwing away a sure thing with Cynthia for a possibility with a woman I had not even kissed yet. In the shower, after getting out of the pool, for the first time in my life, a voice, The Voice, spoke to me: *"You must know, Eric, Cynthia is not a sure thing. There are no sure things in life. But if you put Me at the center of your relationship with Nancy, it will be the truest thing you will ever know."*

I have not heard that Voice since that moment. Perhaps I never will again. But sweet Nancy and I were married fourteen months later.

The message in the shower remains a defining moment of my life. Did God actually speak to me? I am convinced of it, deeply so. Yet in a way, I don't really care about the answer. God is speaking to Nancy and me in our marriage, in our close moments together. The Voice was so right. This is the truest thing I've ever known.

Nancy and Eric Schoeck

Beautiful Eyes

. . . .

IT WAS 1976. At twenty-three years old and very shy, I was lonely and had a difficult time talking with women. A friend of mine had recently joined the Peace Corps and was very excited about it. I think it was his excitement that spurred me on to do the same.

Within months, I found myself in rural Africa, thrown together with a dozen or so Peace Corps workers. The night we arrived, I met and immediately felt attracted to one of my coworkers, a young woman with the most beautiful eyes I had ever seen. I thought to myself, "I've got to get to know this woman."

Then anxiety set in. How would I approach her? What could I possibly say that wouldn't sound dumb?

Usually, at this point, I would give up and make no effort. But something felt different now. My inner urge to meet this woman with the gorgeous eyes was simply too strong to ignore.

I walked over to her. My heart was racing wildly. She smiled and said hello.

I nervously smiled and said, "Hi, where are you from?," and immediately thought, what a stupid thing to say!

She answered simply, "Hood River, Oregon."

My mouth dropped open with surprise. "I am too!"

I could scarcely contain myself. What were the odds of two people thrown together in a remote part of Africa coming from the same small town in the Northwestern United States?

Now it was her turn to be amazed. She lit up like a candle. We talked about all our favorite places in Hood River. Unbelievably, I was a senior while she was a freshman at the same high school, yet we had never seen one another. I felt more comfortable talking with Lynnette than I had ever felt with a woman. Soon we were laughing together as if we were old friends.

Then, as if it weren't enough of a miracle to be from the

same small town, I said something totally unlike me, "Lynnette, don't take this in the wrong way but I need to say you have the most beautiful eyes I have ever seen."

I was immediately embarrassed at having said something so intimate. It could have sounded like the ultimate come-on.

Lynnette smiled shyly and said, "I can't believe I never saw you in high school. I feel the same way about your eyes."

We had been together about ten minutes and yet I knew this was the woman I had been waiting for all my life.

Now, twenty-two years later, we still feel the same way about one another's eyes.

⊚ *Charles Morrow*

The Relationship That Started on the Rocks

· · · · · · · · · · · ·

MY FATHER DIED years ago, and many times I have felt his presence in my life like a guardian angel. He is there, watching over me. I even feel he led me to my husband, Peter.

I was living alone in a little hut out by Medicine Lake in Minnesota after my former husband, Harold, and I had separated. One day my friend Zanna visited me.

"I had a dream about you last night" she said excitedly as she boiled up some hot water for tea. "I dreamed that I was at your wedding."

"What do you mean?" I asked as I reflected back on the

happy day that Harold and I had been married at sunrise on a California hillside.

"You got married to a man named Peter David Longley," she said. "We were all at your wedding."

"But I don't know anyone by that name," I protested. "Besides, I might not like the guy!"

Five years passed, during which time my father had died. I was invited to play some concerts on board the Cunard flagship Queen Elizabeth Two, more popularly known as the QE2. The ship was on her annual World Cruise and had reached Mombassa on the east coast of Africa. I traveled to the ship with guitarist Barbara Polasek. We were engaged as a classical duo. It was hot and humid and we had been traveling long hours. Leaving our baggage at the foot of the gangway we were escorted on board to meet the cruise director. Can you imagine what I felt when I learned his name was Peter Hovenden Longley!

Peter was dark and handsome, a suave Englishman who was much loved by the other entertainers on board. He seemed rather formal as he shook our hands, but I could tell that he was a kind and thoughtful person when he immediately offered to carry our bags up from the gangway to our cabin. In my experience, no cruise director had ever offered to carry my bags.

Naturally, I was curious about Peter, even if his middle name did not match that in Zanna's dream. Two names out of three, I reasoned, was pretty darned accurate. But he was somewhat inaccessible. He seemed shy, and although he was always polite, he didn't say much more to me. Barbara told me to forget about him. She thought he was gay. Then it came time for the final concert. We performed in the Grand Lounge, which was unusual for classical performers. I played my composition "Love Song for the Water Planet." Peter came backstage after the show and simply said, "We've got to talk."

Talk we did. He was deeply moved by my music. It sparked in him a spiritual response, that led him to share a bit of his story with me. He was writing an immense historical novel on the life and times of Jesus and Mary Magdalene, encompassing a very different interpretation of Jesus' message to the world than that which has been handed down to us in Christianity. Peter and I sat up in the ship's nightclub most of that night and he shared many passages with me from his remarkable book. We found we were spiritually in tune with each other.

I did not see Peter again for nearly twelve months, not until I traveled on the QE2 during her World Cruise the following year. Our relationship developed somewhat further during this voyage, still very much centered on spiritual discussions. It did not look, however, that we would enter a romantic relationship even though we both felt a strong love that came from our deep spiritual recognition. He had told me that he was in a twelve-year relationship with a Japanese woman, and that he simply could not separate from her.

It looked like we would perhaps not see each other again. My heart hurt as I recalled Zanna's dream and felt the loss of this possible future. But somewhere deep within I always knew that I would love Peter unconditionally, no matter what.

Wanting to express that love, I composed a piece for him, "Total Freedom in Divine Love," which I later renamed

"Forever," and sent him the tape. I really thought that this was the end of our relationship, but I wanted to express my spiritual bonding with him.

It took an accident at sea to finally bring us together. Two weeks after I had sent the tape, the QE2 sailed into some uncharted granite rocks off Martha's Vineyard. The date was August 7, 1992, and I was in Germany on a concert tour.

That night I had a strange dream. I saw Peter on board the QE2 all covered in mud and lining up the passengers for a masquerade parade. The ship looked like it had been dredged up from the bottom of the ocean. Then the phone rang. It was Barbara Polasek.

"Have you seen the news?" she asked, "The QE2 has had an accident and she's sinking!"

My heart sank as my thoughts immediately turned to Peter's safety. Finally, two days later, I got a message from Peter telling me that everything was fine and that he was now stuck in Boston for a month while the ship was to be repaired. "If you are in the country," he said, "Give me a call. At least we can talk."

A window had opened and I made a momentous decision that changed my life. I faxed the QE2 in Boston and told Peter that I had a concert at the Festival Hall in London the following week, but that I would fly to London from Munich via Boston. I did, and that decision led to us getting engaged the following month and married the next year. I have always said that we are probably the only couple that can honestly say that our marriage "started on the rocks." It can only go uphill from there!

Peter proposed in a Minnesota meadow when we were driving home from a visit to the North Shore of Lake Superior. The sun was setting and a full moon was rising. In the old fashioned way he proposed on bended knee. Naturally, I said, "Yes." It was only then that I told him about Zanna's dream. To this day that dream is recorded in her dream journal. Someday we hope to understand why his middle name in the dream was David.

⊛ *Bettine Clemen*

The Mating Call

. . . .

IT WAS NOVEMBER 1992, and Joshua and I were both students at beautiful Vassar College on the Hudson River in New York State. One day, at three in the morning, I felt stuck writing a paper so I looked outside at the misty rain. I like that kind of weather so, on impulse, I grabbed my coat and went out, hoping to work through my writing block.

Walking in the campus arboretum, I heard a strange sound that could've been a bird, a person, or maybe even a whistle. I stopped and waited, then heard it again. Still not knowing what the sound was, I did something I ordinarily never would have done. I decided to mimic it. As soon as I did, my call was returned from the mysterious source. This went on for a few minutes while I tried to locate the origin of the sound. At the same time, I felt compelled to throw my arms into the air and spin around in a sort of dance, stopping each time I made the sound to listen for a response, then spinning again in the direction of the sound. The last time I made the sound and stopped, my back was facing a street lamp. I heard the sound behind me, turned around and there was a young man coming into the light of the street lamp, also spinning like I was. I stood there transfixed by the image of someone else doing just what I was doing.

As we came into closer proximity, the air seemed alive with magic. We grew silent but kept spinning closer and closer together under the street lamp. We did this for a few minutes, circling around each other while we gazed into one another's eyes. In that moment, I felt that this person I was meeting was going to change my life in some way.

The young man, Joshua, also a student at Vassar, later told me he felt compelled to go out in the misty rain, which he too enjoyed. He described himself as swirling through the mist while making vocal sounds. He too was astounded to come into the lighted area and see me spinning and calling like him. He was struck by how extraordinary the moment was. He also told me later he felt almost hypnotized by my "gorgeous green eyes." Coming still closer together, smiling at one another, feeling in a fairy-tale dreamlike state, he leaned forward and we kissed.

Then we sat on a nearby bench and were soon giggling and talking about what had just happened. It grew colder and the mist turned into a heavier rain, so I invited Joshua to my house a block from campus for some hot chocolate. We got to my house at around four in the morning and talked nonstop until four the next afternoon.

Now married, we often look back on that misty night and remember our mysterious mating call.

ⓥ *Katie Allen*

Saved from the Trash

. . . .

I STILL DON'T know why I placed a personals ad. It just wasn't like me, but I remember the clear feeling that it was the right thing to do. At the end of the ad I said, "If you've never answered a personals ad, and you're conscious and conscientious, please answer mine."

At that time, Donna worked as a medical technician. One day, while sitting at her desk, she happened to glance down at the trash can. Sticking up out of the can was a week-old newspaper. All she could see were the words, "conscious and conscientious." Curious, she picked up the newspaper and read the rest of the ad. She answered the ad immediately.

Meanwhile, I'd received several replies, but none of them felt right so I threw them all away. I felt silly for even running the ad in the first place. Then, a week later, I received Donna's reply. I was struck by the feeling that here was a woman who knew what she wanted. I felt an inner "yes" and excitedly ran to the phone. It was in the middle of the afternoon. When she answered the phone, I blurted out, "Hi, my name is Jim. You answered my personal ad."

Donna had been taking a nap and seemed annoyed at my phone call. "Tim. . . Jim. . . what, who is this?" I had obviously awakened her.

I remember thinking, "Boy, what a grouch!" I threw her letter into the trash and forgot about her.

Two days later, I noticed Donna's letter in the trash and

called her again. This was definitely not like me. I was not known for my persistence with anyone who put me off.

Bracing myself for a second grouchy encounter, I was instead pleasantly surprised. Donna received my call with warmth and friendliness. She apologized for her previous mood. She had been up most of the night consoling a friend. She said she hoped I wasn't offended, and was aware of her tendency to be grouchy when awakened from a deep sleep.

I was very happy I gave her another try. I couldn't wait to meet her, but she put me off for another two weeks before agreeing to meet with me. She was too busy—a potter, she was preparing for a show in a week.

I invited her on a picnic at the coast. I went all out, which was again unusual for me. At the time, I was working for one of the best restaurants in northern California, so I brought along quite an elaborate feast, with many different choices of foods and beverages. Although this was set up to be a picnic lunch on the beach, we stayed together twelve hours talking about everything imaginable. Among other things, we discovered we both grew up in New Jersey, about a half hour's drive from one another. We kissed only once, and that was when I said goodbye. I didn't want to leave her but I knew it was time to go. As I drove away, I knew I had accepted this woman into my heart.

But Donna was still recovering from a relationship and didn't feel ready for a new commitment. After a few weeks, she sat me down and said, "Jim, I feel like you're falling for me, and I'm just not ready for another relationship. I want you to know that I like you, but this just feels too fast for me."

Again, the usual me would have interpreted these words as a rejection, and I would have been out of there in a hurry. But instead, I did something I'd never done before. I listened to words that were painful to hear, took a deep breath, and tried to understand her point of view. For the first time in my life, I didn't react to what could have been interpreted as a rejection. I simply listened to and accepted her feelings.

She later told me that my genuine caring and loving acceptance of her feelings opened her heart in a way she had never experienced before. She knew she had nothing to fear, and could let go of the past. From that day on, we were together most of the time. That was fourteen years ago. We now have two beautiful children together. We are grateful for the loving guidance that helped us grow individually so that we could be together.

⊗ *Jim Connell*

A Surprising Pilgrimage

I WAS WORKING at a great job but felt something missing in my life. A number of my friends spoke about their relationship with God and I realized I didn't have one. I finally quit my job. My plan was to spend a year in Israel exploring my Jewish roots, but first I had the desire to spend a week at Findhorn, a spiritual community in Northern Scotland, and then travel a bit in Europe. I felt clear, however, that I wanted nothing to do with Germany, because of the terrible stories of the Holocaust

I had heard from my Jewish parents and other relatives. I even remember tearing all the pages about Germany out of the tour guide I bought.

At Findhorn, my first roommate was German. So was my second roommate. I started to meet many Germans who quickly became close friends. I ended up staying at Findhorn for three and a half months.

One Sunday, standing in a circle after a meal getting ready to help with cleanup, I glanced to the left and saw a German woman I had never seen before. Inside, I simply heard the words, *"You will be with this woman."*

In the past, I had done the choosing of which woman to be with. This was very different. Mirjam was being chosen for me. But my image of the spiritual journey I was on was a monastic one, so I resisted; I believed a relationship would just get in the way. I waited to see what part of the kitchen Mirjam was assigned to, then I chose the opposite end so, in clear defiance of this inner guidance, I might be able to avoid her.

The next several mornings, I would open my eyes after meditation and Mirjam would somehow be directly in my gaze. I felt like I was basking in her beauty, knowing that this was as close as I was going to get to her. For I was determined to appreciate her beauty from as much distance as possible.

One Wednesday, I decided that I wanted to become a member of the Findhorn community. I was so excited that at breakfast I quickly found a friend and sat down next to him to tell him my decision. Looking past him, I noticed the person sitting next to him was Mirjam. I got flustered, quickly told him the news, and left.

The next day, Thursday, I again was sitting with this friend, and this time Mirjam came over to join us. I stayed only ten minutes. I was still afraid that she would come between me and my spiritual journey.

The next day, I sat next to a woman with whom I had been doing cleanup. Again Mirjam came over to join us. It turned out this woman was Mirjam's roommate. Mirjam and I ended up alone for the next hour and a half. Up to that point, I had been plain scared. Now, however, I was touched by her gentleness. As we parted, I told her I was moving to another part of the community five miles away, and asked her to come over for lunch sometime.

After she left, I regretted leaving it like that, so I went to her room and asked her to go for a walk on the beach with me the following morning. She agreed and, as we were saying goodbye, to my utter surprise, I gently stroked her cheek with my hand. She smiled at me, assuming this must be an American custom. It was something I simply never would have done before.

That night, a friend was having a birthday party. Mirjam was there. After a few songs I asked her to dance. That first dance was amazing—there was so much power and energy between us, people told us it looked like the two of us had been dancing together for many years.

The following day, after walking for a while on the beach, we kissed and both felt the deep connection between us. We were inseparable the next four days. Then it was time for Mirjam to go back to Germany. We both felt it would be good to have some time apart. After all, things were moving much faster than either of us were used to.

Needless to say, I suddenly had little interest in going to Israel. When I finally left Findhorn, I went straight to Germany, the one country I had wanted to avoid most. I realized that to bring God into my heart meant healing those parts of my heart that were closed. And my heart had been closed to Germany—until now.

While meditating with Mirjam in Germany, I had a series of visions. First, our uniting represented the differences we were bringing together, and this would be a healing we could bring to the world. Second, I had a clear vision of us being married. Third, I saw us climbing a mountain together. One step we would be together, then one would help the other climb higher, and that one would then reach down. It was a beautiful dance of helping each other climb a mountain. The final vision was of Mirjam and I in the jungle of the world where we could be afraid and turn to each other, face to face, away from the world, gathering strength from each other and from God. Then we could turn back to back, facing the world again, renewed, radiating our light to help the world. These four visions have become a guiding light for me. We are now married and sincerely trying to live these visions.

I did finally get to go to Israel, but the main reason for my going originally, to establish a relationship with God, had already been fulfilled—thanks to a very special German woman.

℗ *Joel Gilbert*

If From California, Say Hello

WHEN I WAS a teenager, I used to have dreams about a tall, handsome man with green eyes and dark hair. I always imagined myself with this person. When I was nineteen, I married a man who fit the physical description but didn't have the right character. I was in a relationship with someone completely unlike me—different morals, different viewpoints, different expectations about life. I divorced him three years later and spent fourteen years as a single mother of a girl and a boy.

After my divorce, I began to participate in workshops and learned about following my heart. I began to work to make my inner voice louder and give it more respect, to allow God to guide me.

While I was learning and growing, I dated a number of men. I would, however, long for that special person I knew must be out there. I used to sit on my porch and write in my journal things I imagined about him—his personality, his life priorities. I even wrote him several poems as I imagined our lives together. Despite this longing, I learned to enjoy being a single mother and became active in the community. The years were fun and, as I grew, felt very full.

At the end of last year, I began to have dreams that I was in a time of great growth. So I began taking better care of my physical body and lost over fifty pounds. I returned to college and found great satisfaction in learning. Out of the blue, a relative bought me a computer and a client set me up with Internet access.

At the beginning of this year, I had a dream that when a man on the Internet said he was from California, I should say "hello." I would periodically go into the single parent chat rooms and there were a number of men who wanted to know more about me. We talked about our kids and it was a fun way to interact with other single parents a couple of nights a week.

One night, I "saw" a man in the chat room whom I had seen before but thought was from another area of the country. Then someone asked him where he was from and he said, "California." That immediately brought me to attention so, remembering the instructions from my dream, I said "hello" to Benjamin and we instantly connected. Over time, we shared many stories from our past and felt very comfortable with each other. Later, we met and I was blown away by his looks. He was a tall, handsome man with green eyes and dark hair!

It turns out that, as I was having my dreams as a girl, he was living with his family in the same town. In fact, we have lived near each other for much of our lives. When I was sitting alone on my porch writing about my special beloved, he was going through a divorce and getting custody of his two little girls. At one point a few years ago, while I was engaged to someone else, he used to wake up from nightmares that his future partner was committing to another man.

Late last year, before we met, Benjamin began to have visions that a special relationship was heading his way. He was in the midst of another relationship, but it wasn't the soul connection he knew he wanted. So he broke up with her and spent quiet evenings with his daughters. Then his car broke down and was not fixable. He was unable to go on his usual outings, so he started to explore the Internet and discovered the single parent chat rooms and, one night, met me!

Our relationship has transcended any way in which we've behaved before. Usually, both of us are cautious about moving a relationship too quickly, and don't give our hearts too easily. However, we felt so safe with one another that we knew it was meant to be. I began to have dreams about him and he about me. Our children instantly connected with each other and with us. I can't describe how wonderful it is to have finally found the person of my dreams.

We don't live close to each other now, but we've never missed a weekend together. We talk on the phone three to four times per day and never run out of things to say. Either one of us will often bring up an issue the other one has been thinking about. We have decided to not allow fear to stop the flow of our relationship; we just dive in bravely and share what is in our hearts.

People around us assume everything is easy for us. They don't see that it is hard to drive two hours to see your beloved, that it is hard to sometimes go four or five days without touching each other and looking into each other's eyes. Moreover, we have, between us, four children who need substantial time and energy. Following the path of love isn't necessarily easy. Benjamin and I have moved mountains to be together. Once, he drove two hours just to visit for an hour and then drove all the way home.

We planned to be married in June. I never told him that I had, for many years, envisioned a Christmas wedding. Then, a couple of months ago, he said he could no longer stand saying good-bye every Sunday, and asked, "Would you marry me on December 26th?"

"Yes!!" was my exultant reply.

This week, I found my old journals as I packed up to move. I read to him the poetry and writings that I wrote so long ago when he only lived in my heart and my imagination. He was surprised how my written description of him was as if I had already known him. Yes, it's true. I *have* always known him.

℗ *Carolina Willliamson*

It's Never Too Late To Have a Happy Childhood

. . . .

MY CHILDHOOD WAS about survival. Playing, laughing, and pretending were things I watched other children do. I lived day by day trying to escape terror and hunger.

I grew up in the poorest section of a large East Coast city. My mother supported my three brothers and me—and her drug addiction—by prostitution. We never knew our father. I was the third-born son. My oldest brother, by six years, took care of me and my two other brothers. Often he had to take care of our mother as well. The only good thing I can remember about my mother is that she gave half of what she earned from prostitution to my brother. From that money, he bought us food and paid the rent for the lousy shack we lived in. The rest of the money my mother spent on drugs. We commonly saw gunfights, gang killings, and drunkenness.

When I was nine years old, my brothers and I woke up one morning to find my mother's dead body on the floor. She had died of an overdose. Horrified, we went next door for help. My mother's brother finally came and took us to his house. Until I was eighteen, I lived with my uncle, who provided us with food, clothing, and shelter. Although he made sure we went to school each day, he was also an alcoholic and very strict with us. We received most of our support and love from our older brother.

I loved school and did very well. It was an environment that provided safety and consistency. My teachers guided me in the area of computer science because I did so well in math and I received a full scholarship to a university and graduated with honors. Then I got lucky and made a lot of money in the computer industry. By age thirty-five, I had enough money for the rest of my life.

My business success didn't translate over into my love life. My relationships with women were disasters. My longest relationship was three months. Women referred to me as "shut down." After my tenth break-up, I figured a relationship with a woman was impossible for me because of my childhood scars. I invested all of my money and moved to Hawaii. I planned to become a surfing bum and live the rest of my life in solitude, just me, my board, and the surf. Never mind that I'd never been surfing.

My first day in Hawaii, I began to look for a place to live. I saw an advertisement from a person named Lisa who wanted to share her house. I called the number and went over to see the place. Lisa and I felt strangely close right away.

One evening, not long after I moved in, Lisa began telling me about her childhood. She was also the third of four children. Lisa's father was a raging alcoholic who regularly beat her mother and older brother. Lisa learned to be quiet and hide. She started to cry as she told me that she had never been held by her father. I was surprised by my actions: I reached out and held her. She softly cried in my arms. It felt good to be holding Lisa. Tears fell from my eyes. I couldn't remember ever crying before. It was always too scary to cry.

After a while, Lisa sat up and thanked me. She told me that was the first time a man had held her with so much love and acceptance.

Then she asked, "Now tell me about your childhood."

I had never told anyone about my childhood for fear of total rejection. How could anyone not reject me, knowing the situation I came from? Her eyes were soft and caring and, for the first time in my life, I felt safe. I felt a pain in my chest and throat as my built-up defenses gave way to a flood of emotions. The dam I had begun to build as a small child broke wide open. I cried and cried, while Lisa held me and comforted me. I couldn't even speak, so great were the emotions that came tumbling forth.

The next day I could verbalize the pain of my childhood to Lisa. She held me and, for the first time in my life, I allowed myself to feel loved and cared for by a woman. It was the most beautiful feeling I'd ever experienced.

Lisa and I got married several years later, and have been together now for ten years. I never learned to surf, but we swim and play with the dolphins each morning. We've chosen not to have children, as a big part of our relationship is nurturing the wounded little child within each of us. We take turns holding each other and experiencing being truly loved by a safe parent figure. Lisa and I are healing our childhoods. We are also discovering that it is never too late to have a happy childhood.

ⓥ *William D. Jones*

We Never Lost Our Love

. . . .

WHEN I WAS sixteen years old I met my sweetheart for all eternity. Sylvia was fifteen and the most beautiful girl I had ever laid eyes on. We felt drawn to each other like powerful magnets. Attending a small high school in upstate New York in the early 1940s, at first we met at her locker for a few precious minutes between classes. Then I began walking her home. One night she managed to sneak out of her parent's house and meet me at the park. I kissed her for the first time. With that kiss, I felt my heart fly open and I connected with more love than I had ever experienced. I told Sylvia I wanted to love her for all eternity. I offered her my heart to do so as she pleased. Sylvia returned my love a hundred fold. When we were together, it felt as if time stood still and we were perfectly at home in each other's presence.

Many boys my age were mostly interested in trying to have sex with their girlfriends. Not me. I was totally content to hold Sylvia's hand and look into her tender blue eyes. When we did occasionally kiss, I felt as if I went into a deeper world of beauty.

Sylvia brought out the best in me. Before we met, I was an average student with little purpose in life. In Sylvia's company, I became a straight A student and class president. At the age of seventeen, I knew I wanted to become a medical doctor and I knew with certainty that I wanted to live the rest of my life with Sylvia. Sylvia wanted to be with me as well.

For the year that we had been together, Sylvia strangely avoided introducing me to her parents. Finally, she invited me to her house for dinner. Sylvia is Italian and her family was big compared to my quiet family of just my parents and me. Her family had just returned from Mass. Sylvia's father began drinking and asked me what church I attended. I told him I didn't go to church. My father was Jewish and my mother was an was atheist. The room became silent as I spoke. Sylvia's father's eyes grew cold and distant. That night, after I left, he told Sylvia that she was not to go out with me again. "You are only to date Roman Catholics!" His word was final. He was an alcoholic and ruled the family with his anger.

For the year I remained at high school, Sylvia and I maintained a secret relationship. We met in out-of-the-way places and grew deeper in love. One night we made love. Our love and passion for one another was so complete and perfect that I vowed I would never love another woman. I was completely fulfilled with Sylvia and she was with me.

One late evening, we were sitting on a park bench holding each other and watching the full moon. Sylvia's father came up from behind us and grabbed Sylvia. He had been drinking. He slapped her face, then pushed me to the ground and threatened to kill me if he ever saw me with his daughter again.

The next day at school, Sylvia would not look at me. I noticed that she had bruises on her face and arms and her eyes were puffy from crying. She left me a note in my locker saying that she could not see me again. I went from being in a beautiful garden of love to being in the center of an all-consuming fire of anguish. Day after day, Sylvia refused to look at me and returned all of my notes unopened.

My despair grew so great that I dropped out of school and joined the army. I served in Europe during World War II. The war was long and hard, and every day I thought of Sylvia. One day, I received a notice that both of my parents had been killed in a car accident. I felt so alone in the world. That day I made a vow that I would fight for Sylvia and return to her side.

When the war was over, I returned to my hometown. I learned that Sylvia's father had become involved in an illegal activity and had secretly moved the entire family and left no clue as to the new location. I spent a year actively searching, but was unable to contact Sylvia. With no more reason to remain in my hometown, I moved far away.

I finished high school, went to college, and then to medical school. I did my residency in family practice. I loved being a doctor and gave myself into serving others fully. I moved to a small western town and set up an old-fashioned practice out of my house. I visited elderly people in their homes and brought flowers to new mothers. The townspeople loved me and I loved them. Medicine was my life. I tried dating women, but it never amounted to much.

I spent much time and money over the course of the next twenty years trying to locate Sylvia. Apparently, her father was in trouble with the law and successfully changed his last name as well as those of his children. On my fiftieth birthday, I accepted the fact that I probably would never see Sylvia again. I had created a satisfactory life for myself, devoting most of my time to my medical practice. I also became an avid organic vegetable gardener, and took in stray dogs and cats. I had at least four of each in any given period.

Life continued for another twenty years. I kept a picture of Sylvia on my dresser. With the passage of time, I didn't think of her very much, but when I did it was always with the greatest love. I knew that I had experienced true love with Sylvia, and that thought brought great meaning to my life.

When I turned sixty-five, the townspeople worried about my retirement. A new, fancy clinic had been built in town, but a majority of people preferred me. When asked about retirement, I always answered the same: "I'll work until I'm seventy, then I'll retire and do something else." I had no idea what that something else was, I just had a strong sense that I would be called to do something different.

A young couple moved to town and began bringing their child to see me for regular check ups. I liked these two people; they felt strangely like family to me. One day, they called me and said their grandmother was visiting from Philadelphia. She was having chest pains and would I come and check on her. I immediately went and was introduced to Grandma Lewis. She was a frail, thin lady of sixty-nine. When I took her hand to check her pulse, a happy feeling stirred within me. I asked her to tell me of her life. She told me how her family had forced her to marry when she was young. Her husband turned out to be an alcoholic who sometimes beat her when he was drunk. She could not divorce because the church did not allow it. She raised a daughter who was her only joy. That daughter gave birth to this woman and she pointed to her now grown granddaughter. Then she told me her medical history and ended by saying that life with her husband had been so unbearable she often didn't want to live. He died five years before of liver failure and she was starting to feel happiness again in her life.

I decided to prescribe some simple heart medication for her and said, "Well, I'll need your full name. The pharmacy won't accept Grandma."

"My name is Sylvia," she replied with a warm smile.

My heart nearly stopped beating as I looked more deeply into her eyes. "I knew a Sylvia once," I said, "Her last name was Bertucci."

"That was my last name before my father changed it, Dr. Levine," she breathlessly replied.

We stared at each other for a long time and then, in a voice barely audible, she questioned, "Walter?" We threw our arms around each other as the tears streamed down our eyes. We had not seen each other for over fifty years.

Within a month, Sylvia moved from Philadelphia to be with me. The whole town showed up for our wedding. I vowed to be with her every day of my life and love her for all eternity. The townspeople were all crying with joy.

Sylvia and I have now been married for five years. With my love, care, and healthy organic vegetables, Sylvia's health returned. I retired from practice and devote every moment to loving my wife. I have never been happier. People say we act like teenagers because we kiss in public as if no one else is around. The townspeople wonder if I resent all the lost years I had to live without Sylvia. I tell them that I don't have time for resentment because my heart is so filled with gratitude to be with my beloved once again. The years of being apart fade from memory as love fills the very depths of our hearts.

ⓦ *Walter Levine*

Miraculous Healings

. . . .

Sometimes a couple can feel a deep heart connection with one another, their eyes beholding a shared destiny. Usually, however, somewhere along the way the mind realizes it has been excluded and starts to reel, as if to say, "What about me? My ideas count too!" Thus begins the sometimes long printout from the mind's computer:

"She isn't as beautiful and sexy as I had hoped for."

"He isn't very together with his career."

"She doesn't like the out-of-doors like I do."

"He doesn't like to talk about his feelings like I do."

"She weighs too much."

"He isn't attractive enough."

"She already has a child."

"He's too old for me."

81

"Maybe she'll hurt me like my last girlfriend."

"Maybe he'll turn out to be abusive."

"It just wasn't meant to be!"

The mind can always find reasons to avoid intimacy. A relationship can be scary and it is the duty of our minds to protect us from danger. It can be a challenge to keep our hearts open when our minds are offering us rapid-fire information to the contrary. Praying and asking for the guiding hand of love can help tremendously.

The first four stories in this section show the sometimes amazing ways people have overcome doubt in their relationship. They illustrate destiny at work, as well as answered prayers and the spiritual forces that guide our relationships.

Remembering What Is Most Important

. . . .

THE FIRST FEW MONTHS Barry and I were together, I felt as if I were in heaven. I had never felt so totally at home in my life. I listened intently as Barry told me about his life up to the time of our meeting, almost as if he were filling me in on a giant vacation he had gone on. Every detail was of extreme importance to me. He also listened to the stories of my life. Time seemed to stand still when we talked and we seemed to drift to a heavenly place.

Once we went to a dance and held each other close during a slow number. The music ended and the band took a fifteen-minute break. We continued to dance, looking deeply into one another's eyes, oblivious to the absence of the music, the fact that we were the only ones on the dance floor, and even the stares from those who couldn't comprehend the kind of love we were feeling.

One night, we were at our jobs at the school cafeteria. We finished clearing the tables, turned off the lights, and sank into chairs in the far corner of the cafeteria. We were totally alone. The red exit sign cast a warm glow on our faces. As usual we held hands and, between kisses, talked about our lives before we met. Suddenly Barry began telling me about his Bar Mitzvah.

My eyes widened and I couldn't hold back my surprise, "You're Jewish?"

"Of course," was his reply.

It never occurred to me. I was fooled by his name. I thought Vissell was French. And besides, here he was, going to a Lutheran-founded college.

Then Barry asked me, "Aren't you Jewish also?"

"No, I'm not," I answered.

Now it was Barry's turn to show his surprise. He had somehow thought my last name, Wollenberg, was Jewish.

It was a very jarring moment. Our heart connection was so strong and there was such a beautiful energy flowing between us. Amid the feeling of such connection, our minds slowly but surely took over.

Barry's family was traditionally Jewish in both custom and religion. No one in his family had ever married outside of their religion. It was unthinkable. My family was Protestant. Besides spending half of my life in church, three of my cousins had gone on to become ministers. The church was simply my way of life. To marry a person who could not share my feelings about Christianity was similarly unthinkable.

We stared at each other for a long period of time, each of us afraid to speak. Finally Barry spoke slowly, both of us feeling the weight of each word, "Then we can never marry. It wouldn't be right."

There was a long silence as Barry's words sank in. The adult part of us thought in terms of the future, in terms of marriage and family, in terms of culture, and right versus wrong. But there was more to us than our adult selves. We also possessed youthful eighteen-year-old adolescent selves, which soon took over as we realized marriage was a thing adults did and we were still young and could have a lot of fun together. We agreed to totally enjoy each other's friendship. The seriousness of the moment passed and soon we were again giggling together.

After two years, we both realized our relationship had progressed to the point where neither of us could even imagine a future without the other one. Our inner vow to honor our own religion was so strong in us that we each sadly agreed to transfer to different schools. Our minds felt this was the right choice. At different colleges we could forget about each other, meet someone of the same religion, and move on with our lives.

So the following school year, I started nursing school at Columbia University in New York City and Barry went to

Boston University, continuing in his pre-medical education. We spent some beautiful times together over the summer and Barry asked if he could drive me to my dorm to say good-bye. In anticipation of our separation, the drive was slow and sad. We were planning on not seeing or talking to each other ever again. We tenderly held hands and spoke softly and lovingly to each other.

Our minds were convinced that ending our relationship was the right thing. Our parents were delighted and said, "Give the relationship space. Date people of your own religion. Try to forget each other." But our hearts were in deep pain.

Barry entered Boston University where there were plenty of Jewish girls to date. I threw myself fully into life at the Columbia Presbyterian Nursing School. The medical school dorm was immediately next door and I was suddenly surrounded by medical students of my same religion. Though I dated several wonderful young men, that quality of heart connection was not present. I was trying to follow the direction of my mind, but it was difficult.

After one month, Barry called. He told me how much he had been missing me. A joy I had almost forgotten filled my being. "Barry, I thought we weren't going to talk to each other," I exclaimed. My surprise then turned to pure joy. "I'm so happy to hear your voice."

Again, time stood still as we talked for hours on the phone. We made arrangements to see each other. I traveled to Boston and was thrilled to be with Barry again. We realized we couldn't stay apart. Thus began a year and a half traveling back and forth, traveling deeper into our love.

By our senior year of college, Barry and I had more fully entered into our adult selves. Our youthful ability to forget our difference was diminishing. The seemingly insurmountable barrier of religion was once again right in our faces. I would never consider becoming Jewish and Barry would never consider becoming Protestant. Our friends were getting engaged and married. We needed to make a decision about our future. We had no model for a Jewish/Protestant couple. No one we knew had ever even heard of such a match. Our parents were urging us to separate. Our friends thought there was no way we could make it as a couple. We did the only thing we understood to do—we broke up once again.

We planned one final day to be together. We held each other, cried, and expressed our love to one another. We told each other that we would remain in each other's hearts forever. We assured each other that we were doing the right thing. When our time together was up, we kissed and held each other, savoring the feel of each other's lips. Then we said good-bye. I went to my dorm room and cried harder and longer that I ever had. My heart once again felt broken.

The following days, weeks, and months passed by like one painful blur. My mind kept saying, "You made the only appropriate choice. You'll feel better soon." I went out on dates, went to the ocean with my girlfriends, and did every fun thing I could think of. Throughout it all, the pain in my heart grew less and less tolerable.

After three months I could take it no longer. In the middle of one sleepless night, I took the elevator to the twenty-second floor, the roof top of the dorm building. I was alone on the roof looking down on a magnificent view of Manhattan. I stayed up there for hours. I got down on my knees and prayed. I prayed longer and more intently than I had ever prayed before.

I had always felt a deep and personal relationship with Jesus. When my brother joined a fundamental Christian church, he urged me to do the same. Though I loved and honored my brother, his views on Christianity just felt too complicated for my simple devotional nature. For me, Jesus was simply my trusted friend. It was from this innocent place in me that I prayed to Him. I told Jesus that I was willing to sacrifice my relationship with Barry for Him, if this was God's Will. I acknowledged how broken my heart felt. There was a deep, unshakable knowing inside of me that I would never love another man as deeply as I loved Barry. Even given that knowledge, my spiritual path was of greater importance. I saw no way to merge the two. From the depth of my soul I cried out, "If there is any way I can be together with Barry show me the way through a sign. Otherwise help me to accept this path of my religion without Barry." I stayed on the roof until the first rays of sun bathed the Manhattan skyline. I returned to my room and slept peacefully for a few hours.

That afternoon my friend, Sally Bixler, had a surprise visit from her mother. Mrs. Bixler was from a small, central Pennsylvania town. Everything about this sweet, older woman spoke of homespun uncomplicated goodness. She had traveled four hours by bus to visit. Sally and I made a fuss over her arrival. "Why did you come Mother?," Sally asked, hugging her mother.

With a twinkle in her eye and a smile upon her lips, Mrs. Bixler replied, "I was sitting for my usual prayer period this morning. I opened my Bible and a little card dropped out. I hadn't seen this card in several years and I fondly picked it up. As I held it in my hand I heard a voice inside of me say, 'Take this to Joyce today.' So I got on the bus to bring it to you."

She handed me the card. On it was written, "Above all else, love is most important." Mrs. Bixler then reached out to give me a hug. As she did so, I felt myself suddenly enfolded in what seemed like the loving arms of an angel. As she held me, I knew the love that I felt for Barry was most important. I didn't know how we would make our religious differences work in our relationship, I only knew that we would.

While Sally and her mother went off to visit, I ran to the phone to call Barry. Amazingly, he was home. I told him of my tears, my prayers, and of the visit from Mrs. Bixler. He listened to every detail. When I finished there was silence on the phone and then, "Joyce . . . I love you. All I want is to be with you."

The next day we traveled to meet one another. What a reunion! Four years previous we had met in a childlike, innocent way and had ridden on the high of being together. This day we met as adults who had been heartbroken and overcome the obstacles to love. We were united and would never truly be separated again. We were guided back to our hearts by the greatest power in the universe—love.

Ⓥ Joyce Vissell

The Resolution

· · · · · · · · · · · · · · · ·

IT'S NEW YEAR'S EVE, 1937. I am eighteen and I have made an important decision. Tonight, I will break off with Michael after a year of "going steady." I'll wait till the end of the evening though, because it's not fair to spoil our New Year's Eve plans.

I know it's the right decision. Why should I waste my time with him when I don't intend to marry him? I have two more years of college and should concentrate on my education. It's not fair to him either; he should have the chance to find someone else, someone who appreciates him.

Maybe he knows what I have in mind. After all, I have never once said the words "I love you," while he declares his love for me endlessly.

Michael is the opposite of my ideal. Instead of someone tall and dark, he's short and carrot-topped. I want a professional; he's a high school drop-out. And furthermore, my family is on a higher plane, culturally, than his.

The doorbell interrupts my musings. I glance at my watch, 7:45 on the button; that's one good thing about him—always prompt! He's always neat and well-groomed, but tonight he's particularly handsome. There's a knife-edged crease in the trousers of his blue zoot suit. The blue and gold matching tie and handkerchief add a pleasing touch of color to his crisp white shirt. I can see my reflection in his highly polished black shoes. I see my reflection again in this blue eyes as he greets me his usual way, "Hello, prettiest girl in the world." I groan inwardly! It's not going to be easy! We walk the few blocks to the party.

We are six couples who've known each other for years. Half of us are "steadies," the other half just friends. We dance to the records of Benny Goodman, Artie Shaw, and Tommy Dorsey, each couple showing off fancy breaks and dips. Why does he have to be such a good dancer? I think, as we glide smoothly between the others. And he smells so good, a mixture of after shave and maleness.

He tries to kiss me on my mouth, but I turn away in confusion, and his kiss falls on my cheek. "Stop it, willya? Everyone's looking."

"Let 'em look!" he smiles. "It's no secret I love you and wanna hold you and kiss you the rest of my life."

The door opens, and Mr. and Mrs. Miller come downstairs to the basement with platters of food. They're smiling, but their wary eyes dart here and there checking for any improper behavior. Our eyes implore crazy Stanley to behave. Everyone in the neighborhood knows him and feels sorry for him since he lost his mother when he was ten. His father is unable to handle him, and he's constantly in trouble. As soon as the Millers leave, Stanley takes another nip from his flask. His date looks disgusted as he puts on a lampshade and does the hula on the coffee table.

At 11:30, we take off for Times Square. We watch the silver ball drop down from the Times building to proclaim the new year. Oh, the singing, whistling, and kissing! This mass of strangers is united for a few moments with the hope a new year brings!

The last leg of our special evening is the five-cent ride on the Staten Island Ferry. Going to Staten Island is a happy time, with all of us singing our hearts out while the other passengers smile indulgently at us. Returning to Manhattan at 2 A.M., we're ready to call it a night.

Now's the time. "Michael, there's something I must tell you."

At that moment Stanley throws up all over himself and moans, "I feel awful, I'm sick, help me!"

We all turn away in disgust. All except Michael. He kneels beside Stanley and says, "I'll help you, give me your hand."

I watch their hands clasp and the moment freezes in time. I stare at Michael's hands as each hair and vein gets larger and brighter. As I stare, his hands actually appear luminous. I turn to look at the others but they don't seem to notice anything unusual. I look at Michael's hands again and a warmth suffuses my body. I realize that I want to put myself in his hands and share my life with him. I know with my heart and soul that any difficult times ahead will be cushioned by this good man who will always love and cherish me.

Michael helps Stanley to his feet, the light diminishes, and everything goes back to normal. As the ferry slips into the terminal, Michael asks, "Did you want to tell me something?"

I look into his incredibly blue eyes. "I love you." I'm surprised how easy it is to say.

⊛ Helen Vissell

Another Woman
. . . .

SHORTLY AFTER OUR relationship started to become more serious, I started to wonder if this was "the one" for me. My mind became clouded with doubts. Then, one fine Missouri spring day, almost as a direct response to these doubts, I saw Her. The One. As I was walking down the street, the most beautiful woman I had ever seen caught my eye. She was quite a distance away, but I was sure she was everything I ever looked for in a woman. Her figure was trim, muscular, and graceful as she floated across the street in the midday sunshine. She carried herself with such joy and self-confidence. As I walked closer yet, her hair flowed in the warm flowery breeze.

I thought to myself, "I have to meet this woman." Then reality struck as I realized this would never do. After all, I was with Karla and fairly committed to her (or so I thought).

But I couldn't help myself. I took another glance from less than fifty feet away as I neared even closer. My desire overcame me. I relished the fact that soon I would be close enough to actually breath the same air as this goddess. "Forget Karla," I thought, "I have to act on this. After all, I'm not married, I'm a free man."

Approaching her faster now, I envisioned stepping in front of her and yelling from the top of the highest mountaintop, "We were made for each other."

Suddenly, as if she heard my thoughts, this most beautiful woman of my dreams gracefully turned around. As I looked at her face, I could not believe my eyes. I was speechless. Finally, I was able to push past my embarrassment and get out the words, "Oh. . . hi Karla. . . ."

This brief experience did so much to melt away any remnants of doubt about the divine rightness of my relationship with the real "beautiful woman of my dreams." My feelings were so accurate that day. We were made for each other.

☠ *Robert Gitlin*

The Chat Room Miracle

I HAD BEEN dating Alice for about three months and felt a gnawing doubt about our relationship. In most ways she was an incredible woman, extremely intelligent, beautiful, loving, kind, with a great sense of humor. I just couldn't quite put my finger on what was causing my doubt. I think more than anything it might've had to do with "rebound." I met Alice only two weeks after my previous relationship broke up. I remember at the time feeling it was too soon to start a new relationship. I told Alice this and she agreed. We would develop a friendship and not put any attention on romance.

All went smoothly until one night the attraction between us was more than we could tolerate. We made love and soon found ourselves having an intensely intimate relationship. That's when my doubts really came to the forefront.

One evening during the week, Alice called and asked to come over. We were mainly seeing each other on weekends since we both worked hard during the week. I felt hesitant to see her. I was actually looking forward to an evening alone.

I didn't communicate my feelings gracefully. She was pressuring me to come over. Rather than telling her the truth, I said in a voice devoid of love, "Listen, Alice, don't you think we're spending too much time with each other?!"

There was a brief silence on the other end of the line, then I heard, "OK, Simon, I can take a hint." Her voice got louder. "Why can't you just tell me you don't want to see me tonight? Good-bye!!" And then she hung up.

I felt shaken and thought, "That didn't go very well."

Then I was left with my nagging doubts. I walked heavily around the house, looking for something to do. I thought of calling Alice back and apologizing, but I really didn't want to do that, so I didn't.

I sat down at my desk and automatically turned on the computer. As it was running through its startup, I wondered why I had turned it on. Impulsively, I clicked the Internet icon and found myself going into a chat room for singles that I hadn't entered for years. I felt a wave of guilt, realizing the impulsiveness of what I was doing. Reading the conversation on the computer screen, I felt rather foolish and was about to leave when someone new identified herself as Connie and immediately cut through all the usual beginning superficiality of "chat room etiquette."

She wrote, "I'm feeling sad and lonely tonight, but I don't want anyone's pity or advice. I just want to be with these feelings and need to simply have them accepted by someone else."

Her words touched my heart, and I soon typed, "I feel sad

and lonely too, Connie. You have the right to feel anything you feel. My name is Josh."

I wondered why I didn't give my real name.

She wrote back, "Thank you, Josh. I sometimes feel a kind of sweetness to loneliness."

I knew the feeling exactly, and typed, "I feel the same way, Connie. In fact, I feel there is a gift in simply feeling the loneliness. It's almost like the feeling of loneliness is an invitation to understand myself more fully. And if I reject the loneliness, I am at the same time rejecting the invitation."

Connie replied, "Wow, Josh, I've never been able to put that feeling into such beautiful words. Thank you so much. I accept the invitation of my loneliness, and yours as well. May it open doors for both of us."

For a moment I considered apologizing for not using my real name, then dismissed it, thanked Connie, said good-bye, and logged out.

I turned off the computer and lay down on the bed. Connie had no idea how much that brief conversation had helped me. Maybe she never will. She could be from anywhere in the world and I might never be online with her again, but it didn't matter. She had helped me.

Now it was time for me to accept the invitation of my own loneliness. The tears started to flow! Being with my own feelings was being with a special part of myself. My feelings were a special invitation into my own heart.

I lay on the bed for probably half an hour, enjoying the serenity of truly being with myself. It was a kind of self-love I didn't usually let myself feel.

My thoughts then turned toward Alice. I felt how unfair I was being with her. As long as I was trying to use her to fix my loneliness, I couldn't really be with her in her own right. I couldn't see her as the magnificent person she was. And that's why I was doubting the relationship.

I knew I needed to call her and apologize. When she answered the phone, I told her about my experience on the bed, and apologized for the way I had been using her.

She said, "Simon, that makes me feel so good. Now I need to apologize for doing the same thing to you. You were right to keep me away this evening, even though the way you did it hurt my feelings. Still, I was wanting you to take away my feeling of loneliness."

She continued, "I also need to confess something. I got some wisdom tonight from a complete stranger in a chat room on the Internet."

I was getting goosebumps as she continued, "A man named Josh gave me such sweet validation for how I was feeling. . . ."

I interrupted her, nearly breathless, "Was it that the feeling of loneliness is an invitation to understand yourself more fully. And if you reject the loneliness, you are simultaneously rejecting the invitation, Connie?"

"Simon . . . you're Josh. No way! I can't believe this is happening."

"Alice, this is so amazing! I can't believe it either. No, wait, of course I can. How perfect! What an amazing sign!"

Alice laughed, "Simon, can I spend the night at your house tonight? I don't think I've ever felt this close to anyone in my life, or so complete in my own life."

While I waited for Alice to drive the few miles to my house, I silently gave thanks for this evening's miracle . . . a miracle with the power to dissolve doubt.

℘ *Simon Areeze*

. . . .

All good relationships will be challenged at times. The purpose of relationship between two people is to love and believe in oneself and one another, to help and support one another, to open to and receive the love from one's partner, and to therefore grow together. An easy or contented relationship is not necessarily a good one, as the couple may be avoiding necessary lessons. Growth, change, and expansion are also "meant to be."

When challenges or suffering arise in relationship, it is important to know that there is help available by the same loving guidance that brought the two of you together. The willingness to ask for that help is an important part in receiving. It is also important to know that challenges in the relationship do not mean you have a bad relationship. It means you have a growing relationship. The loving hand of guidance can use these periods of challenge to bring healing and spiritual closeness.

There are often unexplainable forces that guide two people through all the obstacles that prevent them from having a deep and fulfilling love. Meeting is one thing, but staying in love may be quite another. All couples know those times in a relationship when it seems the end is in sight, when nothing seems to be working, when you look at your partner and think to yourself, what are we doing together? The following stories show the magic that removes obstacles to intimacy, the "coincidences" that guide couples back onto the track of closeness, the mysterious forces that redirect partners to the highest priorities of life, the importance of love over things, careers, roles, or self-images.

. . . .

Healing from Tragedy

. . . .

WHEN I WAS forty years old I had resigned myself to the fact that I would never marry or have children. I became a second-grade teacher in a poor area of a large East Coast city. I loved being with the children. They were my happiness and fulfillment in life. I had always wanted my own child, but had given up since men didn't seem to like me very much. My social life on the weekends revolved around my parents, aunts, uncles, cousins, and siblings.

One evening I stayed late to decorate the classroom for a Halloween party the next day. These children didn't have much magic in their lives and I wanted the room to be a surprise when they walked in the next day in their costumes. I only meant to stay until six so I could get to my car before dark. However I got so carried away decorating that it was ten before I locked the room and left. I felt happy inside as I imagined the children's faces lit up in wonder as they walked into a magical world.

I was feeling so light and happy that I forgot to take the usual precautions of leaving the building when it is dark. There is a nighttime janitor who will walk you to your car, but I forgot to call him. I was almost to my car when I was violently attacked, beaten, tied up, and raped. Words cannot describe the pure horror of the experience.

I was found several hours later by a man who happened to be out walking his dog. I was taken to the hospital and treated. Even in the middle of the night, my entire family came to my side. Yet despite my pain and anguish, my main concern was for my second-grade students and their Halloween party. I cried about it so much that two male cousins agreed to take time off from work and be in my classroom in the morning to give the children a great time.

The experience of being violently raped was devastating to me. In the weeks that followed, I only felt safe and peaceful when I was with my classroom children. I loved them so much that in their presence I could forget the horrible ordeal. Every other minute, even in my dreams, I was haunted by the memory. I was so on edge that several weeks after the rape I began throwing up almost everything I tried to eat. My mother took me to her doctor, hoping, I think, that he would give me a tranquilizer. He ran some tests on me.

After an hour he gravely walked into the room where my mother and I sat. He asked if there was any man I had had intercourse with in the past three months. The truth was I had only had one consensual sexual experience in my life, and that was ten years before.

His next words came with difficulty, "Connie, you are pregnant from the man who raped you."

I felt like I had fallen into an unreal world. The words I had most wanted to hear the past twenty years, that I would have my own child, came under the worst possible circumstances. While my mother and the doctor discussed the speedy necessity of abortion, I stared off into space. Finally the doctor shook my arm to get my attention saying, "Connie, I can send you to a colleague of mine who can do the abortion right now.

I have already called and set up a time for today. The sooner we take care of this the better."

While I continued to stare into space, my mother got directions and prepared to take me to the other doctor. Suddenly I stopped her and said, "No! I must think about this." My mother and her doctor were shocked and told me there was nothing even to think about. Abortion was a routine procedure in the case of pregnancy by rape. It was usually done the very day it was discovered. I insisted on having some time to think about it.

I went to the place I feel the happiest, my classroom. I dismissed the substitute teacher and sat on the floor with the children and told them my favorite fairy-tale. The children were so good and at the end of the day, for some unknown reason, they all lined up to give me a hug. As the last little one departed the door, I knew I wanted the keep the baby. I felt that a child would bring healing to the most horrible experience of my life. With full confidence and conviction I called the doctor and canceled the abortion.

My family has always rallied around one another. However, the decision to keep the baby brought anger and distance from everyone. No one supported me. They thought I had gone crazy. "Nothing good can come out of a violent rape!" they said to me over and over again.

Everyone was concerned that the rapist's evil ways would come into the baby and I would be cursed for life with a horrid child. Instead, I felt that this baby was coming to me to bring healing. With the decision to complete the pregnancy I felt very peaceful and was no longer obsessed by recurring memories of the rape.

My classroom children were the only ones who were supportive and enthusiastic when I told them I was having a baby. They made pictures for the baby and were continually bringing in presents. I made summer plans to visit my grandmother who lived in Holland. She was the one member of my family who supported my decision.

The school year ended and there were tearful good-byes to my classroom children. I was six months pregnant and each child wanted to pat my rounded belly. My family seemed relieved to see me leave for Holland. They couldn't get past their feeling that I was making a terrible mistake.

My grandmother met me at the airport. She was an active eighty-six-year-old. Her European warmth and welcoming love encircled me right away. For the first time since I decided to keep the baby, I felt loved unconditionally by an adult. I cried in her arms. Grandma wanted me to live with her and have the baby in Holland. The decision to stay came very easily and I settled into the quiet, peaceful life of my grandmother's home.

A week after I arrived in Holland my grandmother's gardener, Willem, came to the front door to announce he would begin working. He was carrying an adorable little girl. Willem and I stood transfixed with each other for several moments before he broke the silence, explaining his little girl's name was Miep and she was almost two years old. She came with him to work and played quietly in the garden. I felt an almost instant attraction to both of them. Willem asked how far along I was in my pregnancy. When I told him six months, tears formed in his eyes and he turned away. That afternoon I went out and played with Miep while Willem worked. No words were exchanged.

The next week I had a lunch all prepared for Willem and Miep and we had fun eating together in the garden. Willem and I talked very little. Most of our conversation revolved around Miep. I offered to watch her for him while he worked at other gardens. He gratefully accepted. Miep and I spent every day together and after two weeks she started calling me Mama. I felt I had never loved a child as much as I loved her. I wondered why her mother didn't watch her more often. That night when Willem came for Miep I had dinner all ready for him. Grandmother was at a concert.

As Miep slept on my lap after dinner, I asked Willem to tell me about her mother. Willem's eyes filled with tears as he began his story. He loved his wife very much and together with Miep they were very happy. His wife was three months pregnant with their second child when she was in a fatal car accident. A drunken driver collided head on with her. She and the baby died instantly. When he told me the date of the crash, I gasped and burst out crying. I cried for a long time and Willem held my hand. Finally I was able to tell him that the car crash took place on the exact date I had been raped. "This baby is from a violent rape," I tearfully explained. Willem held me and told me that he thought all children were a gift from God. He reaffirmed my feeling that my baby was coming to bring healing.

After that night, Willem, Miep, and I spent every possible moment together. It seemed fate had brought us together and all three of us felt the incredible close connection. Miep gave voice to our feeling by calling me "Mama" over and over. In my last month of pregnancy Willem proposed to me. I joyfully said "Yes!" for I knew I truly loved him. We had a quiet wedding, with Grandmother and Miep as our only witnesses.

Willem owned a small house in the country which I moved to one week before the baby was born. Gerde, my sweet angel, was born into a sea of pure love. Willem pressed her little body to his chest and repeated over and over, "My darling daughter I love you!"

Five years have passed and I am still in Holland. Miraculously, our two daughters, Gerde and Miep, look almost like twins. They're both beautiful and have angelic natures. Gerde does not know the story of her conception, but someday I'll tell her as much as I feel she needs to know. For now, they both see us as a family living together in love.

℗ *Connie Van Dam*

Finding Our Own Way

· ·

AFTER OUR WEDDING, Barry and I moved to Nashville, Tennessee, where he was a first-year medical student. We settled into a simple life with Barry going to school and studying late into the night. His only day off was Sunday. I worked as a public health nurse with the poorest of the poor. We took great pleasure in the little time we could be together.

I began attending a Presbyterian church in Nashville. Barry

did not feel comfortable at the services so I went alone. Since Sundays were his only days off, I hated to leave him. So I went to church less and less and soon not at all. Barry had difficulty attending the temple since he needed to study Friday evenings. We didn't have spiritual direction beyond our own religions, so gradually we shut down our spiritual sides.

One and a half years later we moved to Los Angeles where Barry could attend the University of Southern California Medical School and I could attend graduate school. Seeking to fill the spiritual void we turned to drugs, mostly marijuana and psychedelics. Since we were in school, our drug use was minimal. Still, though we didn't know it at the time, we were attempting to fill a spiritual void that could never be filled with drugs.

The vacuum in us was growing all the time. We repeatedly tried to fill this with drugs and an increasingly wild lifestyle. The heavenly feeling from which we married was steadily crumbling. As unstable as our lifestyle was, we always honored the sacred vow of monogamy. One day Barry broke that trust and had an affair. I walked out of the relationship that night. There seemed to be nothing to hold us together anymore. I sadly thought as I drove away from Barry, "Maybe all those people were right. Maybe our interfaith marriage was doomed to failure."

After I left, Barry went through a major change in commitment, and we were able to come back together, but just barely. We needed help, but didn't know where to turn. Our relationship hung together by a mere thread. We loved each other but were lacking a very important and yet undiscovered ingredient.

I mistrusted Barry and felt unsafe. He needed to be trusted again and missed my love. We each sought from other people what we really needed from each other. Barry spent more time with his male friends, while I chose to be with my best friend, Dawn. I was trying to receive from Dawn what I desperately needed from Barry.

One weekend, Barry was free from medical responsibilities for the first time in several weeks. We could be together. Instead, I chose to spend the weekend with Dawn, even though I knew this would hurt him very much. I went to Dawn's house with our golden retriever. Bokie was more like a child to me than a dog. Since I felt so insecure in my relationship with Barry, I counted on Bokie's steady loving presence. He was never far from my side.

Dawn and I were talking and as usual Bokie was lying next to me. Dawn's roommate came home and let in her German shepherd. The dog instantly attacked Bokie. Bokie was not a fighter and took a thoroughly submissive stance. The German shepherd seemed like he was trying to kill Bokie. I became hysterical and reached for the shepherd's collar to pull him away. This was a bad move. The dog attacked me and bit deeply into my hand. His owner finally got him outside.

I went to an emergency room and was told it was nothing to worry about. Back home sixteen hours later, my right hand contracted into a painful claw. Barry took one look and said, "Let's get you to the hospital right away."

The attending physician said I could lose my hand because an infection from the bite was spreading to the bones. I was immediately wheeled in for an operation and emerged with both arms immobilized by needles, tubes, and IVs. I had to stay in the hospital four days. I found myself in a room by myself feeling totally helpless. Barry walked in and I cried, "I need you so much."

"I'm here for you," he smiled. My expression of needing him helped to open his heart, and the woundings of the past several months seemed to melt away as he held me close. Because of the affair and my leaving, Barry had realized his need for my love for the first time in our relationship. Now it was my turn to let myself once again feel my need for his love.

Then Barry was asked to leave the room by a hospital official who needed forms and procedures signed. He was gone about an hour. In that hour, something very significant happened. Minutes after Barry left, a man walked into my hospital room. He said he was a chaplain but he had no religious collar or identifying tags. I had not signed a religious preference form and had only been in the hospital for several hours. How did he even know I was there?

With piercing blue eyes he looked at me and said, "This accident can be the beginning of a whole new life for you."

I just stared at the man. I felt very peaceful in his presence. He then asked permission to say a prayer for me. Bowing his head, he asked for help for not only me but my marriage as well. He was gone as quickly as he came.

I lay there a long time wondering who that man was. How did he know my marriage needed help?

Barry returned and I told him what had happened. "Maybe that was your guardian angel," he half-jokingly suggested.

Barry came to the hospital every morning, during his half-hour for lunch, and at the end of his day of work as a medical student. He tenderly fed me, washed my face, brushed my hair, and supported me in every possible way. We quietly talked about the affair. I shared my hurt and he shared his pain. He said he never imagined his actions would hurt me so much and I finally believed him.

Day by day, as my wounded hand was healing, we were also healing the wound between us. When the nurses, doctors, and assistants saw us in the room together, they left us alone. There was sacred healing happening on many levels, and everyone seemed to respect our privacy.

On the fourth day, the doctor removed my bandages, drainage tubes, and IVs. I had my hands and arms back and, more importantly, I had my beloved back. We still had more healing to do, but we were communicating again and had rediscovered how important our relationship was to us. We walked out of the hospital holding each other tightly. We vowed to do what it would take to get our relationship on a good track.

When I was fully recovered, Barry got some days off from school and we took a little backpacking trip in the mountains north of Los Angeles. Sitting by a quiet flowing stream, we gently held each other and savored our time alone. We both knew we had almost lost each other, so to have found our way back was all the more precious. We read from *Be Here Now*, by Ram Dass, and our hearts were opened to our next step. We realized we needed to find God together, to find the highest truth that would be common to both of us. We needed to find the spiritual cord that threaded itself through all religions, to make our spirituality the rock upon which we would build a new relationship. We also knew we could no longer continue taking drugs. We needed to find a new way to get "high" together, a way that would deepen, rather than erode, our relationship. We also saw that we needed to return to the sacred place of monogamy in our relationship to truly build our trust.

Sitting by the stream in the peace of the woods, we began our spiritual journey together. We did not know how we were going to do this, we only knew that now our spiritual life together had to be our priority. I thought about the mysterious visit from the clergyman in the hospital, the possibility that he was an angel in disguise, come to help open my eyes and heart. I especially remembered how he prayed for me—and us. So for the first time in our relationship, we held hands, closed our eyes, and asked for help. We committed ourselves to growing spiritually as a couple and asked for guidance and direction. That simple act has been the most significant step we have ever made. Our request opened the door and we were led to beautiful, heart-centered teachers and events in the ensuing years. Our newly joined spirituality became the most solid, important part of our lives, helping and sustaining our relationship.

❧ Joyce Vissell

Asking For Forgiveness

BRAD AND I met in high school when we were sixteen years old. I was tall, thin, had long blond hair, and made extra money by modeling. I knew I was attractive and I could date anyone in the school. I dated the class president and various sports heroes. I found them all to be self-centered. Brad was different. He was a simple boy who loved nature and children. He seemed to like me for who I was, rather than desiring me for my body. We took long walks and enjoyed just being together. By our senior year of high school, I knew I was in love with Brad. He was my best friend and in his presence I felt secure and at peace.

I was voted the queen of the senior prom as Brad stood proudly by my side. While cameras were flashing, he whispered in my ear, "You'll always be the queen of my heart, not because you're so pretty, but because of your beautiful heart." Later that night Brad asked me to marry him after he finished college. I had never felt happier.

On the outside everything in my life looked like a fairy-tale. On the inside, however, there was plenty of pain. My father, a well-respected and very wealthy lawyer, had sexually molested me when he got drunk until I was fourteen years old. My mother never said a word to protect me, even though I tried several times to let her know what was happening. I hated them both and wanted desperately to get out of the house. Brad went away to a prestigious college and I went on to a modeling career. I got an agent and began traveling fast to stardom.

Brad and I were in constant communication and visited as often as we could. I moved out of my parent's home and saw them as little as possible. Just as we planned, Brad and I were married when he finished college. We had a picture-perfect wedding. No one knew how painful it was for me to walk down the aisle with my father, for I had never told anyone about the incest. I was afraid people would think I was dirty and bad if they knew my shameful secret. I felt that if Brad knew he would never be able to love me. I smiled my winning smile as I walked down the aisle with my father. People thought we looked so darling together as loving father and daughter. Inside I felt revolted to be that close to him. I was good at acting, however, and no one knew.

Brad went on to become an elementary-school teacher in a poor neighborhood. My father thought he was crazy. "Why settle for such a lowly job when you could make so much more money at a different career?" my father argued one night. I honored and respected Brad for his choice. He loved kids and wanted to make a difference in these underprivileged children's lives. I kept climbing in my career. I was making very big money. Then I got pregnant by surprise. Brad would not even talk of having an abortion. He told me he'd love me regardless of my decision, but his vote was to have the baby.

My agent freaked out, "Debbie, pregnancy is like suicide to your career right now! Wait several more years. You can't afford to do this to your body at this time."

I contemplated the decision for weeks. In a year or two I could be a top model. Yet my heart was calling me to have the child. My heart won! I kept the baby and my belly grew. My modeling career, as I knew it, was over.

Marie was born into loving, happy arms. Brad worked at school and I stayed home with Marie. I nursed her and cared for her, and for the first time in my life I allowed myself to gain a little weight. I never felt so peaceful and contented in my life.

I felt I would live my entire life in this joy, but life had other plans for me.

After putting off my parents for a year, I simply had to agree to let them visit. They had moved 3,000 miles from us. The distance had been a relief to me. Now they were coming to see Marie. I felt so anxious the weeks before their visit. During that time, Brad often questioned me, "Debbie, why are you so upset? Your parents will only be here for two days." I couldn't answer him, but I felt like a volcano about to explode.

My parents arrived and my mother fussed over Marie. My father had brought his own alcohol and made himself a drink. I was all right until he started to get drunk and then reached out and took Marie on his lap. I flashed to the first time my father had touched me sexually. Seeing my innocent Marie sitting on his lap brought back that terror. All the fear and harmfulness of his actions began to rise to the surface.

Fortunately, Marie started to cry and I rushed her out of the room. I didn't let my father near her after that. The visit was soon over and they were gone. But in their place were all the feelings I had successfully hidden for years. I was in so much pain that I began to drink. "Just a beer or two," I assured Brad. "After all, beer is good for a nursing mother."

The beer gradually turned into a six-pack which gradually turned into wine or hard liquor on top. When I wasn't drinking, I was having flashbacks of my father sexually molesting me, which led me back to alcohol to cover up the intense pain.

Brad was greatly distressed about my drinking and insisted I see a counselor. I agreed to go but was afraid to talk about the real issue. At the end of the hour, I was shocked when he suggested I might have been sexually molested as a child. I panicked and never returned. I was determined to keep my secret. I was convinced Brad would never stay with me if he knew my father had slept with me probably hundreds of times. I took to drinking more and more.

One day Brad returned from work to find two-year-old Marie crying in her crib with a very wet and soiled diaper. It was obvious she had been there for many hours in great distress. I was drunk and passed out on the couch.

When I slept it off, Brad told me he and Marie could no longer stay with me unless I agreed to either get professional help or go to AA. I refused both. Brad and Marie moved out that night. I fell even further into alcoholism.

Brad filed for divorce with full custody of Marie. I felt so ashamed of myself I couldn't even fight back. I wasn't granted visiting privileges and I didn't ask for them. Instead I turned to drugs as well as alcohol to numb my pain. I had plenty of money left from my modeling career to support my habit. I rarely was sober.

Three years passed like a blur. Perhaps half a dozen times I called Brad, usually while drunk, to ask about Marie. He was polite but quickly got off the phone. He ended each conversation by asking me not to call.

One night I overdosed at a bar and was rushed to the hospital. I was in there for one week and no one visited me. I had no close relationships. Without drugs or alcohol in my body, the pain of my past rose to the surface in its full intensity. I wanted to die. Lonely and deserted in my hospital room, I cried out one night for help. A sweet, older African American nurse's aide came to my side. This woman had so much love that when she put her large arms around me something broke inside of me. I cried and cried as she just held me and kept repeating, "God loves you."

I told her how I'd ruined my life and wanted to die. I told her about my father sexually molesting me night after night and how I'd lived in pain and fear. I shared about Brad and Marie and how I was so ashamed of myself that I hadn't even tried to see her for three years. I told this dear woman everything and she held me throughout the night. When there was nothing else to say she told me that I have a God in Heaven who loves me who would help me if I asked. Right there she prayed for me. I felt peaceful for the first time since Marie was born.

In the morning I was ready for professional help. I signed myself into a residential treatment program. I started doing the twelve steps. I also started talking about my childhood and the many sexual encounters with my father. It felt good to finally let the secret out. It felt good to feel my anger toward him. I committed myself to recovery.

In time I was able to leave the program and live alone. I got a small apartment by the university and began taking classes to become an addiction counselor. I began working out and eating healthy food. I got a part-time job modeling sports clothes for a catalog. This was a real come-down from my former modeling career, but the people were nicer. I attended AA meetings several times a week.

I was in recovery for one year when I knew I needed to call Brad and apologize for all the pain I had caused him. This was so hard, I kept putting it off. Finally one night I dialed his number and a little girl answered. My heart pounded wildly. "Is this Marie?" I asked in a shaky voice.

"Yes it is," was her sweet reply.

"Could I speak with your daddy please?" I asked, barely able to get out the words.

"Hello," came a familiar kind voice.

"Brad, this is Debbie. . . ."

The voice immediately got colder and interrupted me, "Debbie, I thought I told you never to call here again. . . ."

"Brad, please give me a few seconds of your time. I called to apologize for all the pain I caused you. I'm sorry. I'm in recovery now."

There was a long silence. Finally he spoke, "Debbie, thank you for calling. Marie and I have started over. She's six years old now and doesn't know you. I'm in a new relationship. I need to go now."

Suddenly there was a dial tone. I expected somehow to feel better than I did at that moment. A terrible pain washed over me and I called my sponsor right away. I cried for hours and hours and thought I might never stop.

I didn't call Brad again for a full year. I became stronger in my recovery and found I had much to give to others in pain. My courses were going well and I was on my way to getting a degree. I felt proud of myself. My modeling career was paying well and I was able to buy a small cozy home. As part of my healing process, I furnished one bedroom for Marie. I fixed it up like a magical land. I bought special dolls and toys and had a beautiful wooden dollhouse with electric lights made for her. Every day I spent hours in this room fixing up the dollhouse and adding glow-in-the-dark stars on the ceiling. I often imagined the happy day when I could bring Marie here.

When I next called Brad, I felt strong. I again apologized to him and told him I needed to see Marie. He agreed to first meet with me one week later at my house and then decide if he would let her see me. The night of our meeting, I found myself choosing my favorite dress to wear and spending extra time on my hair. I looked in the mirror and observed that, while I was pleased with the way I looked, I was more pleased with who I had become.

The doorbell rang and I ran to answer it. Brad smiled when he saw me. His face could not hide the surprise he felt. The last time he saw me was the day after I had passed out on the couch five years before. He didn't expect to see such a dramatic change in me. I felt in charge of my life and proud of my recovery process. Brad looked kind as always.

We talked for hours that evening. I shared my entire story with him, especially the part about my father's abuse of me.

"Oh, Debbie, why didn't you tell me?" Brad kept saying over and over.

I told him how even in my lowest days I still had thought of him and Marie and sent them my love. He shared with me his pain from being away from me. He hadn't been able to continue with teaching and had started a business at home so he could be with Marie. He convinced himself that he loved his new partner and wanted to get married. Then I had called to apologize. When he heard my apology, his heart opened and he knew that he could never marry this other woman. He didn't really love her because he had never stopped loving me. They broke up soon after. It was then that Brad started telling Marie for the first time that she had a mother.

"From that time on, Debbie, Marie talked about you every day. I didn't know how to reach you so we just waited. I had to be sure you were really in recovery before I agreed to bring Marie to meet you."

I took Brad up to the room I had created for Marie. It was obvious to him how much I loved the child when he stepped inside.

Brad agreed to bring Marie in two days. "For her sake, I'll stay with her and only let her stay for one hour."

I could tell he was very protective of her. I agreed. Before Brad left he gave me a hug good-bye. It felt so good to be in connection again.

I thought of nothing else except for seeing Marie. Finally the moment arrived and seven-year-old Marie entered my life again. The last time I saw her Brad was taking her away from our home and she was crying "Mommy, Mommy, I want Mommy." Now a sweet little child walked in the door holding her daddy's hand. I knelt down to say hello. I resisted the urge to hug and kiss her. She clung to her father. She had changed so much and yet, looking into her eyes, I could see so clearly my dear little daughter. It was obvious by her manner, dress, and hair that Brad had taken meticulous care of her. There was a strong bond of love between them. I took them both up to

But this awakening needed time to fully become a part of my life. And here I was, throwing myself into taking care of so many others' serious needs. My inner child steadily slipped back into hiding.

One Saturday morning that I happened to be home, I had an experience that changed everything. We had hardly connected that morning. Joyce was up long before me. By the time I got up and dragged my exhausted body from the bed, she had meditated, eaten breakfast, and was preparing to leave to do some errands in Portland. All I could manage was a feeble, "Good morning," as she headed for the door.

For some unknown reason, Joyce stopped, turned around, and came back to me. She threw her arms around my neck and pressed her body close to mine. She seemed to be holding on to me in a way that she hadn't in a while. It felt good. I felt how much I was missing our closeness. Then she pulled away slightly so she could look into my eyes.

"Barry," she said with that unmistakable tone of the little girl who was needing love and, unlike me, was willing to ask for and receive it, "I need you so much. Can we be together this afternoon?"

"Sure," I said, feeling slightly more alive in my still-tired body.

Joyce smiled. I've always loved her smile. It seemed to light up my day more than the sun, which was seldom seen in these gray Pacific Northwest days.

Then she was gone out the door. "Drive carefully," I called after her. That was silly. She always drives carefully. I hadn't said that in a long time. Oh well, I thought, it's always good advice.

I made myself a cup of tea and went into the spare bedroom we had made into a sanctuary. There were flowers on the little table. Joyce has always loved flowers. I sat on my favorite cushion and closed my eyes. Meditation seemed to come so naturally to Joyce. For me, it was a different matter. While Joyce was attracted to a devotional approach, often feeling God as a loving Mother or Father, I preferred aiming for stillness, following my breathing as a way of quieting my mind. God, to me, was that rare and somewhat elusive feeling of deep peace.

This morning my mind seemed to be on a racetrack. My thoughts were chaotic, not making sense at all. I remember thinking that perhaps I was spending too much time with psychotic patients, and their minds were having an effect upon me.

I brought myself back to my breathing, trying yet once more to quiet my mind. Suddenly I had the image of Joyce in a head-on car collision. It was an awful sight, with twisted metal and blood. Now I'm really crazy, I thought, and tried to get the image out of my head. But it wouldn't leave. I tried focusing more intently on my breathing, in a desperate attempt to erase the vision, but without success. Then I said to myself, in a rare moment of surrender to what is happening, OK Barry, just flow with it. Don't fight it. I gave in to the images. . . .

Meanwhile, Joyce was driving through the hills on small country roads. She was listening to her favorite music cassette on the stereo. At the same time she was trying to decide how she wanted

side. I'm now more a part of you than ever. In love, we're eternally joined."

Of course, I thought, feeling myself waking up as from a bad dream. Joyce has always been such a deep part of me, and is now even more so. It felt like a shaft of light penetrated the blackness of my loneliness. I need never feel alone again. It was a moment of clear spiritual truth.

Then a second thing happened. I remembered that all this was just happening in my mind, that I was sitting on my meditation cushion in our spare bedroom. The images were so real they had swept me away into another reality.

Waking up more fully, I felt so much joy that Joyce was still alive. We still had our lives to live together, a whole world of experiences and adventures that would deepen our love. How could I ever take this woman and this love for granted again? I resolved inside myself to remember this experience, so I would never make anything else more important than love. I would always remember that Joyce and I are united in our hearts. And I would make it safe for the little boy inside me to ask for and receive love from her, from the infinite source of that love, and from everyone.

When I opened my eyes, the flowers on the altar were once again a display of Joyce's living presence in my life.

In the moment before impact, Joyce could now see a group of wild teenage boys in the car ahead. In the last possible moment, the driver swerved and narrowly missed hitting her. They were playing a dangerous game of seeing how close they could come without hitting her. They were seeking thrills.

Joyce came to a complete stop, leaned on the steering wheel, and started crying. She felt badly shaken. It was a long time before she felt capable of driving again.

When I heard the car pull into our driveway, I felt elated. I ran out to greet a still shaken Joyce. She ran to greet me. We held each other a long time. She told me what had happened and how scared she felt. I looked deeply into her eyes and then said, "Joyce, our love is the most important thing in the whole world to me. I hope I never again take this love for granted. And one more thing: I'll always need your love."

Her smile said more than any words could have in that moment.

℗ *Barry Vissell*

Visitors on the Mountain

. . . .

MY WIFE, JUDY, and I were married in 1982. I had been a fearful child and was shy and withdrawn in college. I had never really had a girlfriend until graduate school when I met Judy. Judy drew me out right away. In her presence, I could laugh and talk freely. With Judy I felt happy for perhaps the first time in my life. After two years, we married and moved to Seattle while we worked in an engineering firm together.

Judy and I both wanted children so we began almost immediately to try to conceive. Month after month we tried, only to be disappointed. After three years we grew very discouraged

You'll never amount to anything." My therapist helped me to finally feel my pain and helped me to begin to heal.

Four months after my backpacking trip Judy found out she was pregnant. Our joy was extreme! I went out and bought two baby swings and a jogging stroller built for two. Judy laughed at my seeming irrational behavior.

Several months later the doctor confirmed that we had one healthy baby. I could not believe it. "I know there are two in there Doc!" I said with certainty.

No, he maintained, helping me feel the one head and listen to the one heartbeat. Judy didn't care. She was so happy to be having a baby. For me, I just couldn't let go of the feeling that something wasn't right. I continued to buy two of every baby item. Judy finally asked me to stop, saying that it was upsetting her. She asked me to just accept that we were having one baby. In my heart I kept feeling two. The image of those two beautiful, angelic beings on the mountain would not leave me.

Judy began to labor three weeks earlier than expected. We rushed to the hospital. After an uncomplicated labor our beautiful baby daughter was born. Tears streamed down my face as I saw her for the first time. The doctor asked me to hold my daughter while he attended to Judy. As I was looking into my baby's eyes I heard the doctor exclaim, "Oh my, what a surprise! Here comes another one!"

Ten minutes later a second baby girl was born. My heart felt as if it would break open in joy and wonder. All these months the first baby had hid the presence of the other, saving the grand surprise for the end. As I held my two babies I was reminded of the time I had first met them one year ago on the mountain. They had guided Judy and me back together and had guided me to seek the help I needed for my own healing. They are ten years old now and continue to teach us in the ways of love.

© *James MacMillan*

Lost in Paradise

. . . .

MADELEINE AND I dreamed of moving to Montana for a long time. Even though we had high-paying jobs in Los Angeles, me in the computer industry and Maddy in fashion design, we were burned out. The lure of the "Big Sky State" had been with us both ever since we had backpacked there on our honeymoon five years before. Finally, we took the plunge, quit our jobs, sold most of our fancy furniture, and headed north in the springtime with a trailer-load of "essentials."

We found a place to live in a magnificent, mountainous area at the end of a private road. The house was a bit run down, though livable But it was the land that we fell in love with, twenty acres bordering a vast national forest. Wildflowers were bursting out everywhere from lush meadows and hillsides. It looked like the paradise we had always dreamed of.

By fall we were starting to realize that paradise can never be a place outside of ourselves. The harsh realities of living so far away from the rest of the world were taking their toll. We had each hoped we could still earn a living using our skills, even from this out-of-the-way place, but it wasn't working out as

death out there somewhere, or being dinner for some large predator. I wished most of all that I had not taken the relationship for granted these past months.

In my desperation, I decided to pray for God's help in finding Maddy. I felt awkward. Prayer was not something I was comfortable with. Sometime before the dawn, I must have dozed in the chair.

My eyes opened to the first light in the sky, and I felt more clear and alert than I had in a long time. I suddenly and unexplainably "knew" where Maddy was. But the problem was that the "knowing" didn't have a "where" attached to it. It was simply an inner feeling. I would have to trust my instincts.

Running out the back door, I quickly climbed the hill and stood for a moment on the top. I felt a strong pull to the left and started down to a small valley we had explored once before. Once in the valley, I turned to the left again to follow it down to a small stream. I knew how much Maddy loved to walk along streams. But this didn't feel right. I had made the decision based on reasoning, not inner "knowing." •

I abruptly turned around and walked up the valley toward the mountains. The going was much rougher, not the kind of walking my wife tended to do, but it felt right. I was now climbing up a steep ravine, calling out her name. I can't tell you how new this was for me, to be so deeply trusting an inner feeling rather than trying to figure things out with my rational mind. Could it be that God was answering my prayer and directing me to find Maddy?

Just then I thought I heard a distant call. I held still and called out to Maddy. Yes, I heard it again. It was her!

In fifteen minutes, I rounded a corner in the ravine and there she was, huddled at the base of a tree, her knees drawn up inside her down jacket. I ran up to her and held her close to me. She was cold and shivering, but she was alive and very happy to see me! I wrapped her in my jacket. She explained that she had fallen and badly hurt her ankle. She had tried to walk but it was too painful.

I told Maddy about my night, about my prayer, and about how I felt guided to find her. Then I said, "Nothing is more important to me than our connection. I vow to you I'll never ignore our relationship again." Maddy smiled and then snuggled closer to me. She was cold and in pain, but at the same time happy.

It took hours, and the help of three other men, to get Maddy back to our house, then off to the nearest hospital. Her ankle wasn't broken, just badly sprained. We got back home in the middle of the afternoon.

Sitting on the couch in our warm home, sipping hot tea, Maddy said, "Jerry, I'm so sorry for the hurtful words I said to you yesterday."

"Never mind," I tried to stop her, "I know you were just angry. I'm just so happy we're together again."

"Yes, I was angry," she continued, "But all night in that cold ravine I kept thinking about what I had said, about feeling like I was drowning but you didn't notice. All night I hoped that I was wrong. And now I know, I was wrong. Not only did you notice, but you cared for me enough to let your heart guide you to find me. Your finding me was the miracle I've been needing all these months."

Over the next several weeks Andrew was diagnosed with non-Hodgkin's Lymphoma, stage 4. The cancer had metastasized into his bone marrow. He was given a 30 percent chance of survival. The cancer was fast-growing, and he needed to begin treatments immediately.

He had minimal health insurance, and this was a grave concern to him. I still worked at the university and had good coverage. A neighbor who also worked at the university suggested to me that I marry Andrew, because then my insurance would cover him. That idea had not occurred to me, and although I had occasionally thought about getting married, I felt in no big hurry and we had never discussed it.

For the next couple days the idea of marriage stuck in my mind. I knew I loved him, and although it didn't seem like the best reason to marry, it did seem like it would solve a lot of problems. I knew that he would never ask me to marry him under these circumstances. So I approached him with the idea. We talked about it for a couple days, and then decided to do it.

Although he was in shock in dealing with his disease, Andrew drew on his ten years of experience of emergency training in staying calm in a crisis and establishing a strategy. Our immediate reaction was to rally forces from the community around us. Andrew needed support from as many people as possible, and we realized getting married would be a significant step in forming our team. We had been operating as a team for almost a year, and it was natural to work together in the face of emergency. We called our closest friends, and established a group to help spread and gather information. One of the main people on our team was Andrew's old friend Jack

Miller, who also owned a jewelry shop. Andrew was buying our rings from him when Jack wisely asked, "Andrew, are you marrying her for love or insurance? You better get that straight."

Andrew looked at Jack, then looked at his own heart, smiled and answered, "Love."

We had a ceremony on a hill overlooking the ocean in a place Andrew thinks of as "God's Country." Only our minister and dear friend Kat, her partner Al, and our dog were in attendance.

My health insurance covered the most aggressive treatments available at the time, and after two months of chemotherapy, Andrew entered the Stanford Hospital isolation wing for a month of radiation and bone marrow transplantation. Andrew maintained an incredibly positive attitude. He visualized himself on a "self-rescue," which meant that after rescuing countless people as a lifeguard, he was now using his skills and experience to save himself.

Our marriage was a huge turning point for both of us, and we were amazed at how it felt like our love deepened almost immediately. It became a bright spot in a time of hardship. It was truly a bittersweet and romantic time. I drove to the hospital every day, where I would wash my hands for three minutes and don a gown and mask so I could be with him. Andrew joked about how he couldn't recognize his nurses because he didn't see anyone's nose or mouth for a month. Although he couldn't see my nose or mouth either, he loved to recognize me by my eyes. While he was in the hospital we dreamed about our future together, read sailing magazines, and thought about buying a boat.

whom I loved dearly. My sister had been helped by attending one of Joyce and Barry Vissell's workshops on "Living from the Heart." She wanted me to go with her. Larry was very support-ive and agreed to watch the children for the weekend. Reluctantly I went. I felt very shy the first day and, in my usual behavior, I withdrew from the group. I didn't want to go back for the last day, but my sister really encouraged me to go.

Joyce had us close our eyes for a meditation. I couldn't fol-low the meditation, but I did feel more peaceful than I had in a long while. Suddenly I heard her say "You have a loving Father/Mother/God that will never leave you and will always love you. You are a precious child, cared for and protected." In that instant I realized that I have a Father in Heaven who will never abandon me and that it wasn't my fault when my father left. I began to cry out loud. I felt so embarrassed but could not stop the tears. All the years of holding back my pain came to the surface. Charley Thweatt, the musician for the weekend, sang a beautiful song. Barry and a few people in the group came close to me. I felt surrounded by love. I then shared with the group about my father leaving when I was ten years old, my feelings of guilt, and the decision I had made to always be "good" so that I would never be left again. I also talked about the seven years of knowing Larry was having affairs and how I was afraid to speak to him about it. Barry and Joyce talked to me about the importance of saying no when something wasn't right. They also spoke about respecting myself and honoring my feelings. These were all new concepts to me. Charley sang another song and for the first time in my life I prayed and asked for help.

The next week I lay in bed alone. Larry was gone. At one in the morning, I heard the door quietly open. Larry was home. I crept down to the living room. The smell of perfume filled the room. I flicked on the light. Larry was startled to see me. As I looked at him, I felt a strong energy move within me. I normally felt weak and defeated when he came home like this. This time I felt strong energy welling within me and in a loud voice I didn't even know I had I said, "No, Larry! I will not let you do this anymore. You are hurting me and the children."

Larry later explained to me that when I commanded "No!" there was a brilliant flash of light. In the center of the light, he saw above my head a huge, powerful-looking being. In that instant, the atrocity of his actions shook him like an earthquake.

He stared at me in disbelief, his face white as a sheet, then he started crying. Before long, he crumpled to the floor in tears. He cried and cried and kept saying, "I'll stop. I'll get the help I need. Please give me another chance."

Larry went into counseling for sex addiction. I continued to learn about self-respect and honoring my feelings.

That was ten years ago. Now we have six children and a strong monogamous relationship. Love needed to be firm to guide us solidly together again. Not only did I find my voice, but I also found my Father, my Real Parent.

⊛ Audrey Clark

convention. Doris was very attractive, but even more, I loved how independent she was. She seemed so solidly centered in herself, so able to take care of herself, so different from both Barbara and Virginia. I was swept off my feet by her vivacious personality, not to mention her physical charms. We got married after knowing each other three months.

I soon learned that, underneath Doris' dynamic, independent exterior hid a little girl so desperate for love that she dared not show herself. She and I were an unhealthy combination. I hid my need for love in work. She hid hers in not needing anyone. Before long we were living totally separate lives under the same roof. Doris and I were married for two years. I finally suggested she move out.

Partly it was three failed marriages. Partly it was a midlife crisis. Mainly it was the despair I was feeling, the gnawing feeling that I might never find inner peace. I took a leave of absence from my practice. I felt like an alcoholic who has tried and tried to cut down on his drinking and finally simply has to quit altogether and get help. I had tried for so many years to cut down on my workaholism. Now I needed a total break from work. The longest I had ever gone without working was a seven-day vacation with Virginia.

I joined a men's therapy group, where I finally met other men working on their own workaholism. They became my best friends. We supported one another in our recovery process. We traveled together. I had enough money from investments to not work for many years if I needed that.

Perhaps most importantly, I learned step by step to value myself and my life. I learned to take care of my body by eating better and exercising. I learned to take care of my mind by reading self-help books. I learned to take care of my soul by engaging in a more active spiritual life. Things were starting to look up.

Curiously, along with all of this, I was feeling less and less desperate for a woman. Although I looked forward to some day sharing my life with a lover, it felt so important for me to be alone in this time.

I remember one night reading about the importance of asking in prayer to be guided to a true spiritual partner. Something struck a chord within me. I closed my eyes and surprised myself by asking God to guide me to a woman. Not just any woman, but a woman I could travel with on a shared spiritual journey. That part felt very important to me. Then, in some place of deep and sure knowing within me, I knew it would happen soon.

About a week later I received in the mail an invitation to my high school's twenty-fifth reunion. I looked at the date and immediately checked my planner. It wouldn't work. I was already enrolled in a weeklong retreat, an event I was much looking forward to. I tossed the invitation in the garbage. Anyway, I wasn't interested in seeing those friends from the distant past, all of whom I had lost touch with.

As I stood up from my desk, however, I suddenly wondered if Barbara would be there. Although I hadn't seen or heard from her in many years, I felt convinced that she would still be happily married all these years. That was just who she was. But there was no way I would change my plans.

Then, two weeks before my retreat, I found out it had been

once and stood up to hug me. Then she looked confused and said, "Kyle, you're the last person I ever expected to see here. Aren't you too busy to be coming to a high school reunion?"

I laughed, then added, "Tommy told me you weren't coming. It's so good to see you. You look fabulous."

I became aware of many eyes staring at us, some recognizing us and others distracted by us. I took her hand and said, "Can we go outside and talk for a few minutes?"

She left with me. We sat on the steps in the warm sun. Barbara's face looked more beautiful and radiant than ever.

"Barbara," I began soberly, "I need to sincerely apologize to you for my workaholism, for taking you for granted the years that we were together. I've learned a lot since then."

I told her about my healing journey. Then I asked about her husband and family.

She looked thoughtful, "I've been divorced for five years. Our two children are adjusting okay. It's just that I hadn't learned my lesson after being with you. I went from one workaholic to another."

Then she smiled warmly, "It feels so good to hear your apology. I never dreamed I'd hear that from you. I have an apology too. I'm so sorry I didn't stand up for myself more in those years. I just didn't know that I deserved love and attention from a man. I gave up and turned to food instead."

I couldn't believe the feelings that were arising in me. It felt unbelievably good to be in Barbara's presence. She was the same, yet also so different. Her inner calm spoke of years of growth and wisdom. It had been over ten years since the divorce and here she was, more beautiful than ever.

I simply had to say it. "Barbara, you have grown so much. You're so beautiful."

She actually blushed, then smiled warmly and replied, "And you, Kyle, I never in a million years thought you would transform your life like this."

I'll never forget the feeling of sitting there on the steps outside Central High's auditorium. We were looking into one another's eyes, and the warmth of the morning sun couldn't match the warmth I felt in my heart to be reconnected with this soul. The love that we had from the beginning of our relationship was there in that moment, but there was so much more. It felt like a new love, a deeper love, a kind of recognition that is possible between two souls who have loved one another for a very, very long time. It was a love that has known the pain of separation, the overcoming of major obstacles, and then the triumphant return and celebration.

When our lips met again after all those years apart, I felt what I had been missing in my life. At the same time I felt like we had never been apart.

That high school reunion was twelve years ago. Barbara and I are married again. We have found a most precious gem in our love. It's like being in both an old and new relationship. Old because of the familiar feelings and reawakened love. And new because of the growth that happened in each of us during our time apart.

I'm amazed at how close I feel to her children and how much I feel like a father to them. The other day at dinner we got laughing over my "fourth marriage to my first wife."

I have often remembered that night I prayed to be guided

to a woman with whom I could share my life, as well as the feeling of how soon it would happen. Little did I know where that guidance would lead me.

® Kyle Seligman

Rediscovered Love
. . . .

MY HUSBAND, LEO, and I met and married in 1948. Leo was a pre-law student, a football hero, and the most handsome man I had ever seen. I was a psychology student and very interested in human growth and development. I had dreams of becoming a psychologist.

While Leo attended law school I worked at a secretarial job. I became pregnant with our first child the year Leo passed the bar exam. Becoming a psychologist faded into the background.

Within six years we had three children. Leo became a successful lawyer. He spent long hours at the office and often worked on the weekends. Being a mother to three little children kept me very busy. Sometimes while changing diapers or doing a load of dirty clothes, I would remember my dream of becoming a psychologist. I would realize with sadness that my dream was fading, while the reality of motherhood was taking over.

Leo was offered a position by a very prestigious law firm in California and we moved when our children were entering the preteen stage. Leo worked more and more and I busied myself with parenting activities. Notwithstanding the loss of my dream, I still enjoyed every aspect of parenting and that became my total focus. Leo and I both knew our relationship was suffering from lack of attention, yet we both kept focused on our individual activities and the children. Occasionally we took a family camping trip in the mountains. These were the best times we had. We bought a white camper which we named "Traveler." When we were outside in nature away from phone and office, our family felt close and connected. At home my needs for connection and fun were met through being a mother. I was very close to my children.

Then came the day that our youngest child went off to college. That night, Leo and I sat down for dinner and realized we had very little to say to each other. We had become strangers.

It was finally time for me to pursue my long-held dream. I began a masters program in counseling. While I was studying and attending workshops on personal growth, Leo was winning difficult cases. He didn't want to attend workshops with me and I wasn't interested in his lawsuits.

One night we discussed getting a divorce. We had grown so far apart that divorce seemed the most logical route to take. Later that night our eldest child called to announce that he proposed to his girlfriend and they wanted to marry soon. His light, joyous mood contrasted sharply with the seriousness of our conversation.

I slept in my son's room that night. I cried a long time, feeling how hurt our children would be to have us divorce. I prayed and asked for help for Leo and me. Eventually I fell asleep. When I woke in the morning I had an irresistible urge to go camping. Our family had always been happy on camping trips. Perhaps, I thought, nature would bring some joy back into my life. Surprisingly, Leo was open to the idea. He had deep circles under his eyes and I could tell he, too, had not slept well. We were both suffering in our own private worlds. On a whim we packed up our old camper. Leo was scheduled to be out of town on business. He called and canceled. My school was in break so I had two weeks off. We decided to take a few days and go to a place we had enjoyed with the children. Outwardly we told each other there was no hope for our relationship. Inwardly we each held a tiny hope.

Packing the camper took longer than we thought and we didn't start out until late afternoon. Though it was November, the weather had been sunny and warm and we packed clothes for moderate temperatures. While driving we began to talk about the divorce again. As angry words flew back and forth, we didn't realize we had taken a wrong turn and then another. Years of hurt and disappointment were being expressed as we drove. We didn't even notice when we turned onto a road marked "Closed in Winter."

It started to snow. I was crying and Leo was yelling when the camper started to bounce. We realized we were off the road but there was nothing Leo could do about it. We came to a stop under a tree. He put the camper into reverse, but we were stuck in mud under a thin layer of snow.

We got out and inspected the situation. It was snowing harder now. Getting back inside, Leo tried several more times to get out, but without luck. We were badly stuck.

We resigned ourselves to our fate, climbed into the camper and soon were quite cozy. "We'll be rescued in the morning," we both agreed confidently. I made a nice warm dinner and we ate by candlelight. We were hopeful to be back home by the next day. That night we slept together under the warm blankets I had brought.

We woke in the morning to a near white-out blizzard. No one was going to find us today and we weren't going anywhere. We had enough food for perhaps four days and enough propane for heat for maybe six days. I made oatmeal and we sat close together on the little couch in the camper. We discussed our argument from the night before. Rather than continuing to blame each other, we began to listen to one another's hurts and disappointments. There was so much we hadn't understood. I didn't know that Leo had felt left out by the closeness between the children and I. He didn't understand how much I wanted to be with him and how lonely I felt. He felt unappreciated for working hard to support the family. I felt he didn't understand how much work it was to raise three children with so little help from him. We apologized to each other and asked for forgiveness. We communicated more in that one day than we had in the entire thirty years of our marriage. We held each other as we went to sleep that night. We were confident that a snow plow would find us the following day.

We woke to more heavy snowfall. Leo made pancakes with a grand flair. We pretended we were in a fancy restaurant. We passed the time by remembering all the funny things the children had said or done. At one point I started laughing so hard and Leo leaned over and kissed me. We hadn't kissed in many years. Leo had gotten into the habit of sleeping in his office at home. It had been longer than we could remember since we had been affectionate with each other. We were silent and looked at each other for a long time.

"I've missed being with you, Nancy," he gently said as he reached over and kissed me again. We made love that day in a long leisurely way. Each touch and caress brought memories of times when we were lovingly connected.

As we later lay together in the stillness, Leo held my hand and whispered in my ear, "Nancy, I love you. Can we start over again and get remarried rather than divorced?" How I had longed to hear those tender words from Leo. I snuggled close and we fell into a peaceful sleep.

The next day was cold, overcast, and clear enough to see our surroundings. It had snowed four feet. We surveyed our surroundings. For the first time we realized that we were not on the road going to our traditional family camp spot. That road was always kept plowed. We had never been on this road. Leo studied the maps for hours calculating time traveled and distance. With shaking hand and fear in his voice, he pointed on the map to a small road clearly marked "Closed in Winter."

"Nancy, I believe we are here." The map told us that roads closed in winter are not plowed or maintained. Leo estimated that we were fifty miles away from a plowed road. With the equipment we had, that was much too far to walk. Our mood shifted drastically as we realized our chances of being rescued were slim. Right then a helicopter flew past. By the time we got out of the camper into the open, it was gone. Leo explained to me, "That helicopter was probably checking to make sure the road was clear of cars. Our white camper is under this big tree and most likely invisible by air." Our big chance at rescue had just left!

All our energy now went into survival. I had a large red sleeping bag in the camper that belonged to our son. Using old sock and rags I sewed "HELP" onto it. We carefully put it out on an open piece of the road. Securing that blanket and keeping it free of snow became our main concentration. We rationed our food. We used the heat sparingly.

Ten days went by. Our food and heat were gone. All we had now was the snow outside to eat. We stayed mostly in bed, where we were warm and comfortable. Several times a day we checked on our "help sign." During this time we had many meaningful talks. We realized how deeply we loved each other. We had let the pressures of career and family life consume us. Our love had always been there, it was just buried under responsibility. Probably a hundred times a day we told each other how much we loved each other. We held hands and touched feet as if our very survival depended upon our connection. We thought of all the times in the past that we had neglected to appreciate each other, and so we took the opportunity to make up for lost time. Each moment of each day we were faced with the possibility of not surviving. Though there was a tragic sense to the situation, there was also a serene peace that passed between us. We had found our love again, and that was worth everything.

Two more weeks passed without food or heat. We kept the camper door clear, we checked on our "help sign," and we ate snow. We talked about death. For the first time in our relationship we prayed together. We talked to God together throughout the day and felt a loving closeness and comfort surrounding us. I could see into Leo's soul, into the essence of who he was, and I loved him unconditionally. He returned the same love to me.

Four weeks had passed since we had gotten stuck, and we had been without heat or food for almost three weeks. Leo was no longer able to get out of the camper. It took great effort on my part to check on our "help sign" and clear it of snow. Leo had health problems from the past which were now manifesting. I knew he could not survive much longer.

One evening I brought our last remaining candle and placed it by Leo's head. "I want to get married all over again," I quietly but eagerly announced as I reached down to kiss him. He opened his eyes and smiled weakly. As he lay on his pillow, we got married to each other in the highest way. We promised to love and honor each other's soul in the afterlife.

Leo slept peacefully on his pillow. Every ounce of my being felt in total love with him. As I listened to his breathing, I took out my only piece of paper and wrote to our children. I told them how we had lived our final days in peace and in love, and were connected in a way we had never experienced before. I told them how much we loved them and that our love would be with them forever. I put the letter on the table. That night as I crawled into bed I knew that Leo had little time left to live. I decided that I would stop eating the snow and checking on our sign. I wanted to die with Leo.

The following morning I woke with a start. Leo weakly opened his eyes, but could no longer speak. I held him close. I intended to hold him every second before he died. I told him over and over again of my love.

Suddenly I heard a noise outside. Before I knew it, a helicopter had landed and three men were making their way through the snow drifts toward our camper. I could hardly believe this was actually happening. I opened the door and stared into the faces of three young men. They looked like angels. They knew just how to care for us. Within a short time we were both in stretchers flying to the nearest hospital. My only request to our rescuers was that I wanted my stretcher close to Leo's so that I could hold his hand.

It took time, but Leo did regain his strength. He retired from law practice and we spent every day together. We are now in our seventies and not a day goes by that we don't remember our ordeal in the snow. We are grateful to have survived, but even more grateful that love guided us back into each other's arms.

☘ Nancy Whitmore

Fulfilling Our Dream

. . . .

I WAS DATING a man named Kevin. Although I felt very attracted to the way he looked, I wasn't really attracted to him as a person. He was the type I could be best friends with but not someone I wanted for a partner. He felt the same about me. We felt such an unusual connection, though, that we continued to date.

One day, Kevin's identical twin brother, Larry, came to visit. He was on the soccer team of the college which was challenging our college. I went to the game with Kevin and enjoyed watching Larry play. He was a natural athlete and, even though he was a sophomore, he was clearly the best on the team. After the game, the three of us went out to dinner. In every way, Larry looked just like Kevin, but looking into Larry's eyes I saw a man I could live with the rest of my life. Larry was also very attracted to me and, at the end of dinner, Kevin suggested that I visit Larry at his college ninety miles away. We both looked at Kevin in astonishment as he simply stated, "Patricia and I are just friends. I can see something more with you two."

It took just one visit with Larry to know we had found our mate. We traveled back and forth as often as we could over the three remaining years of college. Larry's skill in soccer was so great that he was approached by professionals. He declined a fabulous offer to follow his dream of becoming a doctor. He wanted to be a pediatrician. Larry loved kids, and often told me that his dream in life was to marry me, have two boys, and do everything together as a family. I gladly shared Larry's dream, and we married two weeks after graduation.

Larry was accepted by a good medical school and we moved. I worked as a personal assistant to an executive in a large company. My work was challenging and exciting, but what I really wanted was to be a full-time artist. Larry assured me that when he finished with his medical training, I could devote my time to art. He was very busy with school and hospital work, but when I did see him it was pure magic. We'd meet for lunch occasionally and kiss most of our allotted half hour. I knew that even though he was so busy, his love for me was the priority in his life. Every day, Larry talked about wanting to have children. He kept saying that he saw us with two boys.

Kevin, meanwhile, met and married the woman of his dreams and moved close to where we lived. Like Larry, Kevin loved children and dreamed of having a family. Kevin's wife, Margaret, and I grew to be best friends. The four of us did things together and definitely were a close family.

Kevin had mumps as a child and doctors warned him of the possibility of sterility. He and Margaret tried for four years to have children and finally accepted the fact that they could not have children naturally. They finally approached Larry with the idea to save his sperm and let the doctors do in vitro fertilization using Margaret's eggs. It felt right to all four of us.

Larry began saving sperm and taking it to the sperm bank at the hospital. Two attempts were unsuccessful for Margaret and Kevin. Larry continued to save sperm in case they wanted to try again. During this period, Larry did a strange thing. He took out a very large life insurance policy on himself. I questioned his use of money for something that seemed so unnecessary, but Larry was very firm about his decision.

Two months later, he called me one evening just before he left for home. Larry always expressed his love to me, but during that call he was especially appreciative and loving. The last words he spoke to me were, "Patricia, after all these years, I'm almost through with my medical training. I want to make love with you tonight and call forth our baby." I told him I'd be ready. I lit candles and waited and then received the phone call that changed my life forever. On his way home from the hospital, Larry was killed instantly when a drunk driver hit him head on.

Words cannot describe the anguish I experienced. My only consolation and comfort were Kevin and Margaret. The three of us shared our grief and were a tremendous support to each other.

One month after Larry's death, I remembered the sperm bank and the ample quantity of sperm that he had faithfully collected for Margaret and Kevin. I also remembered Larry's last words to me about conceiving our baby. An idea formed in my mind so powerful that it took over my every waking moment. I wanted to bring forth Larry's baby! I would try in vitro fertilization using Larry's sperm. Larry's life insurance policy, which he had mysteriously taken out two months before he died, gave me enough money for the rest of my life. I could comfortably stay home and and raise our child without financial worries.

Kevin and Margaret vowed to help me. They even decided to try one more time themselves. A date was set and Margaret and I were to be implanted at the same time. In this procedure, the woman's egg is fertilized by the man's sperm outside the body and then implanted in the uterus. There is only a twenty percent chance of achieving pregnancy. To improve those odds, the doctor implanted three fertilized eggs within each of us. Throughout this procedure, I felt Larry's presence with me.

I could hear his voice over and over saying, "I want to call forth our baby."

The in vitro procedure was a success for both Margaret and me! Margaret was pregnant with one fetus and I was pregnant with two. For the first time since Larry was killed, I felt a surge of happiness grow within me.

Throughout my pregnancy, I felt Larry's arms around me and I could almost hear him whisper in my ear, over and over, "Patricia, I love you and I am coming to you in both these baby boys." I never felt alone in my pregnancy, Larry's love was so present for me.

My twins were born first. Two big, healthy baby boys. I named them John and Peter, after two great men that spread the love of their Master wherever they went. I knew my John and Peter would spread the great love of their father as a blessing to our world. Ten days later, a baby girl was born to Margaret and Kevin.

It has been ten years since the twins were born. I feel so fulfilled and happy with my boys. They are both exceptionally loving and caring toward me and receive great joy in doing special things for me. They both look like Larry in different ways. Peter is a natural athlete whose passion in life is soccer. John is the more sensitive one and loves to play with young children and babies. He says he wants to be a great doctor just like his dad. Kevin, Margaret, and ten-year-old Rose Marie live close by and help me when I need an extra parent. I am now a full-time artist.

The boys' presence in my life can never replace Larry, but they have brought the completion of a dream that Larry and I shared. John recently brought home a picture from school, entitled "My Family." In the picture, Peter, John, and I are standing in a meadow of flowers holding hands. Above us, he drew an angel with arms spread wide and light coming forth from his heart surrounding us. In his childish writing he had printed "My father" over the head of the angel.

℧ *Patricia Parker*

. . . .

*Other persons can provide powerful ways to help us in our rela-
tionships. It could be a teacher, a friend, a spiritual leader, parent, sibling, or child. These people can be used as instruments to
give us direction and hope. By their belief in us we can be brought
out of darkness and confusion into the light. These people are
often beacons of light helping to illuminate our path.*

*After we beseech God to help us with our problems, we often
forget to notice the old homeless man on the street corner who
may be trying to give us the answer to our prayer ("Angel on the
Street"), or the checkout clerk at the food market who has a special message for us, if we are paying attention. Or we miss the
love being offered by a loved one because our eyes are looking to
the sky, waiting for a shaft of light to come from some God far up
above us. God, the Highest Spirit of Guidance, is within all of us,
is Who and What we are.*

*May the last few stories of this section remind us that love is
often passed from one heart to another. There is an old saying,
"love is caught more often than taught." We catch love by making
ourselves ready, by asking for it, by knowing that we deserve all
good things as Sons and Daughters of the Divine Being.*

. . . .

Angel on the Street
· · · · · · · · · · · · · · · · · · · ·

AS FULLY AS I loved Kathy even after six years of marriage, it deeply hurt me to hear her sometimes complain that she didn't feel heard by me. After all, as a psychologist in private practice in New York City, I prided myself on my ability to listen to others. I well understood the concept of the therapist who was paid to listen all day long to patients and then doesn't want to listen to his or her spouse at the end of the day. But I felt I really wanted to hear what Kathy was feeling and thinking . . . at least most of the time.

One evening, after a particularly grueling day with patients, I came home more depleted than usual. Walking into the living room, I saw Kathy sitting on the couch, her eyes obviously red from crying. I remember feeling the strong urge to turn around and walk out of the room. I just didn't want to deal with yet more emotional upheaval.

Instead, I walked over and sat next to Kathy. I tried to summon the strength to comfort her, but I felt hollow inside as I asked, "What's the matter, Kathy?"

She looked up at me through puffy eyes and said, "I feel so lonely."

I knew she was talking about our relationship. I immediately felt defensive, but muttered, "I'm here with you."

The words were nice, but it was a lie.

She looked away and quietly said, "No, you're not. Please go away."

Inside, I felt like exploding. The feeling of rejection combined with the emotional exhaustion of my day was too intense for me to contain. I quickly got up and left the apartment. Walking in the twilight along the Manhattan sidewalk, I felt so many conflicting feelings: anger, sadness, fear of losing Kathy, helplessness.

At a street corner, while I was waiting for the light to change, a man called out to me from the steps of a building, "Hey, buddy, come over here."

I looked over and saw an older man in tattered clothes smiling at me. If it weren't for his smile, I would have ignored him and walked on, thinking he was wanting a handout. But the smile was strangely compelling, so I approached him.

"Yes?" I hesitantly asked.

The smile disappeared and a serious expression came over his face, "You look like a man who is having trouble with his wife."

How did this stranger, this probably homeless vagrant, know what was going on inside of me?

Incredulous, I stared at him and asked, "How did you know?"

"I been around," he started to say. "Some things are obvious if you take the time to notice. For example, I can see you give a lot of yourself to a lot of people. Ain't that right?"

Again I was dumbfounded, "Yes, that's right."

His eyes seemed to pierce right through me as he next pronounced, "Stop pretending to be strong all the time. You need love, man. You need her love, man."

These were the kind of words I had so often spoken to my patients, reminding them of their own needs, reminding them that it was okay to need and ask for comfort from those they loved. Yet I didn't take my own advice. This evening especially I was needing Kathy's comforting more than usual, yet I buried my need under the rug and pretended to want to comfort her. Was it male pride? Was it that I didn't feel worthy of her love? What was it?

The old man laughed out loud as if he was reading my mind and said, "Don't try to figure it all out. Just go back home and let her know the truth—you need her love."

I wanted to ask the man his name, find out who he was, spend more time with his extraordinary wisdom, but he simply smiled and pointed his finger back in the direction from which I had come. I understood that he was skillfully ending our "psychotherapy session," so I took his hands, thanked him, and left.

At that moment all I wanted was to see Kathy's beautiful face. I hurried back to the apartment, raced up the stairs, unlocked the door and rushed into the living room. She wasn't there. I peeked into the bedroom and saw her lying on the bed, still crying. I lay on the bed next to her and whispered into her ear, "Kathy, I'm so sorry I've kept you away from me all this time."

She stopped crying and looked at me, "What do you mean?"

I felt calm and yet just like a little boy as I explained, "So many times I've needed your love and comforting, but have been afraid to ask. I get so caught up in the role of provider, of the strong helper in charge of every situation, that I forget how much I need your caring. Like now, when I see your pain and sadness, I tend to ignore my own pain and sadness. But that's not being honest with you. I really need your love."

Now I was crying.

Kathy smiled and her tears sparkled with a new light. "Morgan," she said softly as she reached her arms around me, "I have so much to give to you. It hurts to have so much love to give and not have it needed."

As I basked in the warmth of Kathy's love, I silently gave thanks to the old man on the street. I decided to find him and repay him in some way for saving my marriage.

But I never saw him again.

℗ *Morgan Hirschfield*

Peaches

· · · · · · · · ·

WE WERE TRAVELING across the country together during summer break, as "just friends." One day in Texas, we noticed peach orchards along the road. We thought about how nice it would be to get some peaches, but our limited student budget did not allow for such luxury. Despite our lack of finances, we pulled over to a small orchard in the middle of nowhere. We got carried away by the beauty of fresh ripe peaches hanging on the trees. Before long we had filled a large paper bag. When we went up to the stand to pay we realized that the amount we picked exceeded our funds. As we were sizing up the situation, the old woman at the stand began talking to us. She grabbed the bag of peaches and placed it in the back of our pick-up truck and then looked deeply into our eyes. We asked her how much they would cost. It seemed as if she did not even hear our question. Then, she smiled and said, "For you two . . . no charge."

We looked at each other with wonder. Free peaches, what a blessing. Then she continued in a very maternal and loving way, "Just promise me one thing. Always be good to each other."

We smiled back as thoughts ran through both our heads, "But we're just friends."

Then, with the gentleness of an angel she continued, "And always remember, when you eat a peach, that once an old Polish woman gave you peaches."

Now ten years later, our third daughter's nickname is Peaches and we always strive to live up to the promise we made to an angel whom we will never forget.

⊚ Robert Gitlin

Miraculous Passages

. . . .

*P*erhaps the most dramatic demonstration of the
power of love can be experienced at the time of the
death of a beloved. Birth and death are two times when
there seems to be a nearness to the heavens, when the angels
appear to draw close to human beings, when the miraculous often
becomes evident. Of course, these spiritual influences can happen
anytime, but there is more often something extraordinary and
even mystical about the events that take place at the time of a
loved one's passing. May the following amazing stories show you
the eternal nature of love, reminding us that the body may die,
but love goes on forever.

Ruby's Message

. . . .

MY WIFE, RUBY, and I had ten incredible years together. Ruby was the center of my life, my best friend, my sensitive lover, and my golfing buddy. The one sadness that crept into our relationship was our inability to conceive a child. We tried repeatedly and spent big money on medical interventions. Finally we resigned ourselves to being childless. We loved each other so much, we knew we could live with this.

Then, on a vacation cruise, a miracle happened. We conceived a child! We were both ecstatic. The pregnancy was like the completion of our happiness. I have always been an overly protective sort of guy, so I arranged the very best care for my wife. I watched over her like a mother hen would her little chicks.

Eight months into the pregnancy, Ruby woke with a start. "Gordon, something strange is happening" she exclaimed. "I need to get to the hospital!"

I moved into action and got her there in ten minutes. The doctors examined her and were concerned. "Quick, get her to the operating room!" they shouted as attendants ran down the hall with Ruby on a stretcher. I ran along with them. Just before she was wheeled in, she weakly looked up and told me how much she loved me. Then the doors closed and I was alone.

One hour later, the doctor found me pacing back and forth. "Sit down, Gordon," he said with a grave expression upon his face, "Your wife had a placenta separation which caused her to hemorrhage. We acted quickly, but not quickly enough. We were only able to save your little girl."

The doctors words hit me like a hammer on my heart. Ruby, my precious Ruby, dead. How could my heart's treasure be gone?

The doctor walked me to the premature nursery and I held my baby. She started crying and I started crying. An automatic numbness came over me after that. I mechanically arranged for the funeral and took care of all the other details. I named our daughter Summer Ruby, after her mother and because summertime was Ruby's favorite season.

I couldn't even begin to make plans. My sixty-two-year-old widowed father had retired from his job as an elementary school teacher. He offered to come live with me for a few years and help take care of Summer. The plan worked well. My dad was great with kids and he and I had a good relationship.

My grief over Ruby's death was huge. I took every class and workshop on grieving that I could find. Had it not been for the presence of my sweet little Summer Ruby, I might have gone mad with grief and pain.

In addition to grief workshops, I also took workshops on dream journaling. I learned to wake myself up after a dream, write it down, and then quickly return to sleep. This process was very important to me, as I occasionally had a dream in which Ruby appeared. I highlighted all dreams with Ruby in pink. These became a tremendous source of strength for me.

Once, she came to me in a dream in flowing white robes and told me how much she still loved me. In another she told me that Summer needed a mother. I wrote that dream down and highlighted it, but I didn't like it. I didn't want to marry again. Ruby was my one true love. For two weeks in a row, Ruby came to me every night and told me that Summer needed a mother.

One day, my dad said, "I've been here for two years now. I love you and Summer very much, but I need to get on with my own life. I've always wanted to go on an extended trip around the world. I want to do this next year before I get too old."

I knew Dad wanted to travel. I guess I just wished he'd always live with me. I knew I could put Summer in day care and she would survive.

That night Ruby again came to me in my dream. This time there was a figure of another woman whom I could barely see. Ruby spoke in the dream, saying there was another woman for me.

I awoke in a cold sweat. Opening my heart to another woman was scary for me. What if that woman died also? Then I would have to feel the pain of loss all over again. As lonely as my life was, I had my dreams of Ruby and my sweet Summer to comfort me.

The next night my dreams were especially vivid. Ruby came to me and again told me how much she loved me. She yet again said Summer needed a mother. She said this was to be the last dream I would have of her for a while. Then she pointed to a figure of a man and told me to listen to him. She slipped away in my dream and a man stood before me. I could see him very clearly and he told me his name. He also pointed to a large table of jewelry. I somehow knew in my dream that he wanted me to meet the woman who made all the jewelry.

I awoke and wrote down every detail, including the man's name and what he looked like. My heart was beginning to open slightly to the idea of a relationship. The possibility of meeting someone new and being in love again was both fearful and exciting.

Though I was very careful to wake after each dream I had, Ruby did not reenter my dreams. However, I had other dreams, some of them with a woman I could not see and a table of jewelry. Though I could not explain it, my desire grew day by day to meet this woman.

Dad moved out to begin his travels. Summer and I were alone now. Weekends I would take her to jewelry shops. I told her I wanted to see the jewelry, but secretly I was wondering if I'd meet this mystery woman. Nothing ever came of this. I bought Summer a bunch of cheap necklaces and bracelets which she wore every day. Friends followed my lead and gave her their old discarded jewelry. Sometimes she wore up to ten necklaces at one time.

We started going to craft fairs and looked at all the jewelry. It was now two years since my last dream of Ruby. Summer was four years old. I didn't even understand why I kept taking Summer to these craft shows. The whole idea of meeting another woman who was somehow connected with jewelry seemed preposterous to me now. The craft shows had merely become a habit. Summer enjoyed them and so we went.

One night, Summer had her first sleepover at her best friend's house. It was my first night away from her. In the quiet of my home I realized how utterly lonely I was. I had made no close friends since Ruby died. I was still living in the memory of our relationship. I wanted to move on, but didn't know how.

For the first time since I was a little boy going to my grand-mother's church, I prayed. I asked for help to move on with my life. I asked for help in finding another partner. For the first time in four years I felt ready to love again.

Two months later, it was close to Christmas and Summer wanted to go to a craft show. She got dressed up with all ten necklaces, several bracelets, and some huge, rather ugly clip-on earrings. She felt she looked beautiful! Hand in hand we walked down the long aisles and displays of crafts. We always stopped at jewelry booths. This time, without seeing it, we walked past a small display of jewelry. The woman called out to Summer, "My, how pretty you look!" We walked back to her table. She admired Summer's jewelry, even the ugly earrings. Then she gave Summer a little crown she had made of beads and feathers. It was a little thing, not worth very much, but to Summer it was the world. I've never seen her so happy with anything.

"Now I can be the queen," she happily sang.

The woman laughed and whispered to me, "Oh how I wish I had a daughter of my own."

I noticed a bored preteen boy sitting behind the display table. She introduced him as her son and explained that he would rather be playing soccer or golf with his friends than sitting at the craft table with her.

Just then, another customer came and Summer and I left. That night, Summer played and played with her new crown. She treated it like her most special treasure. I had noticed that this woman had other, more expensive crowns. An idea formed in my mind to go back and get one for Summer as a present from Santa.

While Summer played at a friend's house the next day, I slipped back to the craft fair and found the woman. As she was all alone and the fair was almost empty of customers, I sat down for a few minutes to visit. I learned that her name was Melissa and that her husband Joseph had died suddenly in a motorcycle accident three years before. She supported herself and her son by making jewelry. She also shared how difficult it was raising a boy by herself. I could hardly believe it but, before I hurried off to pick up Summer, I found myself asking for Melissa's phone number. My heart felt light, my mind was almost giddy, and I sang Christmas songs out loud all the way to pick up Summer.

Melissa and I entered into a wonderful relationship. She taught Summer how to make jewelry and I was thrilled to have a new golfing buddy in her son, Jacob. Times with the four of us together were good too. Melissa and I set a date to get married. Our children were thrilled.

Two nights before the wedding, Ruby appeared to me in a dream for the first time in over two years. Appearing very happy, she was standing with her arms raised as if to bless me. Then she picked up a journal and pointed, as if wanting me to read it. Then she slipped away.

The following morning I told Melissa about the dream. Melissa suggested Ruby might have wanted me to read my old dream journals. I dug them out of my closet. I found the two weeks of dreams in which she wanted me to find a mother for

Summer. Then there was the dream with the man. Melissa's eyes widened as she read with me from my journal, "The man said his name was Joseph and he had short curly dark hair with a mustache. He had a bright smile with two big dimples." Melissa spoke slowly, "This is an accurate description of my Joseph."

We looked at each other in awe. My precious Ruby and Melissa's beloved Joseph had somehow worked together to guide us to one another.

⦿ Gordon Miller

The Good-bye Hug

. . . .

AS A YOUNG father, my dad seemed to have a hard time showing his affection to us kids, but in his later years that all changed. He became more and more demonstrative of his love, but never more so than to my mother. It seemed that hugging her was one of the greatest joys of his life. He hugged her in public just as much as in private, in the morning just as much as in the evening. Sometimes Mom would get embarrassed by his shows of affection, but I could tell she enjoyed it nonetheless.

For most of the last thirty years of his life, my dad suffered from poor health. Toward the end, his heart was failing, along with many of his other organs. Many days it was a chore for him to just get from room to room in their home near San Diego. Even painting in his studio, his passion, seemed to be fading. Still, none of us suspected his time of death was so near at hand.

One afternoon, Dad was watching the Padres, his favorite baseball team, on the televsion in the guest room. My mom needed to run some errands, so she stuck her head in the room and told Dad she was going out. For my dad, there was no coming or going, even the running of a little errand, without a hello and good-bye hug. So, difficult as it was for him to get up from the couch, he stood for their customary hug.

Mom and Dad embraced for a moment and then Dad suddenly and silently fell over backwards, pulling Mom with him. As she fell on top of him, she had the thought, "Michael is playing a trick on me." Dad did have a knack for impish tricks.

She called out, half annoyed, half amused, "Michael, what are you doing?"

There was no response. She looked more closely and saw that he was not breathing. The reality hit home. Her beloved husband had died doing what he loved most, hugging her.

⊗ Barry Vissell

The Best Christmas Present
· ·

CHRISTMAS IN OUR family of four was always a fun time. But Christmas 1996 was tough for us. My sons Shawn and Kevin, both in their twenties, and I were still in shock from the death of our beloved husband and father.

On Christmas Eve, Kevin had to work until 10:00 P.M. Since

he had to go to work again at 6:00 A.M. on Christmas morning, Shawn and I decided that we would open one gift each after Kevin got home and before we went to bed. We then would open the rest of our presents after Kevin got off work Christmas afternoon.

It didn't work that way. We were all feeling a bit blue; we missed our loved one who had always loved Christmas so much; we ended up opening all of our gifts, and it was almost midnight by the time we got to bed.

I was sleeping in the recliner in the living room. Around 3:00 A.M., I was suddenly awakened from a very sound sleep. When I opened my eyes, there was a figure standing by the Christmas tree and looking at me. It took me a moment to realize that my husband was standing there.

I was more thrilled than frightened; this had never happened to me before. As I moved forward to speak to him, he shook his head, smiled at me, and put his finger over his lips in a motion for me not to speak. Then he sent the telepathic message into my heart that he was just fine and was happy, and at peace.

My husband was there only for a moment and never physically touched me. Yet I felt as though he had put his arms around me and given me a special hug, just like the two of us had shared during our marriage.

Suddenly he was gone, and I was left, once more, in the dark. I went back to sleep. The next day, I didn't mention this to either of my sons.

When Kevin came home from work on Christmas day, he came in while I was fixing dinner in the kitchen and said,

"Mom, I have something I want to tell you but I don't want to upset you."

He then said, "Dad was here last night. He came into my room, and I woke up. He was standing there, watching me, and I felt like he was talking to me even though he didn't seem to be moving his mouth. He told me he was happy and that I should help you with the things you need."

Shawn was not home yet, so he knew nothing about Kevin's and my conversation. Later that night, after everything was quiet and we were all sitting in the living room relaxing, Shawn said, "I saw Dad last night. He came to my room about three o'clock this morning and he looked really good, Mom. He would not let me talk and he did not say anything but I felt like he was telling me that things were going to be better for us now."

Unbeknownst to each of us, we three had received a visit from our loved one as our best Christmas gift ever.

℘ *Myrna L. Smith*

Dancing With Angels

ONE WEEK AGO, on December 21, 1998, after the last candle of Hanukkah was extinguished, the evening of the Winter Solstice, I said good-bye to a man I considered my life partner.

My forty-eight-year-old husband Michael entered into a realm of light we had only imagined we would face thirty years or more hence. We had planned on retiring, when the time was right, to Key West, Florida, where we would watch the sunset night after night, never tiring of its splendor. Instead, I will scatter his ashes into the ocean there as the sky turns golden and magenta.

When Michael was diagnosed with Chronic Active Hepatitis C more than six years ago, we were told by a physician friend that the disease was "like rust that eats away at the foundation of a bridge. Eventually it breaks through and destroys the bridge." After numerous rounds of Interferon, excruciating pain that required narcotic intervention, nausea, edema, weakness, fatigue, memory loss, change in mental status, and multiple hospital stays, it finally broke through.

Michael's spirit throughout all this was inspiring. He managed to laugh his way through as much of it as possible and when that didn't work, he was able to cry his way through the rest. I laughed and cried along with him. I reminded him that we were a team and this was the "in sickness" part of the marriage vows we had taken more than eleven years ago.

A few months before he died, he told me that had he known he was going to be this sick, he never would have married me. How lucky for both of us that we didn't know! The truth is, the last six years of our marriage were deeper, richer, and more fulfilling than the first five, because we came to recognize what was important.

In May 1998, Michael was placed on the national list for a liver transplant. We were told that the wait could be up to two years and that 50 percent of the people in Michael's condition die before a transplant. At the time, we were convinced that we would beat the odds. After all, he had purpose, solid spiritual faith, good doctors, a healthy attitude, a nutritionally sound diet, and an amazing support system.

For the past ten years, we had published a magazine called *Visions,* which gave us access to some of the best known healers in the world. When Michael became too sick to work, we transferred ownership of the publication to friends. That was in June 1998. By July, we began the bizarre dance between home and hospital, and by November, Michael entered Thomas Jefferson University Hospital in Philadelphia in a comatose state.

During the forty days that followed, Michael's condition took dramatic upward and downward turns. It was like being on a roller coaster. My spirit followed suit. What amazes me is how strong we can be when called on to do so. I created a healing haven in Michael's room in the Medical Respiratory Intensive Care Unit (M.R.I.C.U.), which I came to call "the miracle unit." Soothing music played day and night. Photographs of family and friends surrounded him. Pictures of Michael as he appeared in healthier times were on the bulletin board so that the staff could view him as a whole person, not just a sickly body to which they tended. Spiritual healing tools and cards from loved ones and even strangers decorated the window sill. Michael was immersed in prayer as it emerged from the hearts of people all over the world. The doctors and nurses, whom I will forever refer to as "angels in scrubs," cared for him with tender loving compassion.

During those five and a half weeks, I sang to him, read to him, and prayed with him, filling him with as much light as I could, urging him to use my energy, certain that God would replenish me. Girded with the strength of those prayers, I stormed heaven, wrestled with God, and prepared to take my husband back. I wrote copious amounts in my journal—letters to God, to Michael, to his anticipated donor and family. I designed scenarios in which Michael would return home to a magnificent party attended by family and friends. Instead, it took the form of a celebration of his life that was his memorial service on Christmas Eve.

Even though Michael was under heavy sedation much of the time, I could feel him communicating with me. I entered his room at five one morning to find his right hand, swollen as it was, in the position of the "I love you" symbol in sign language. That was one of our special ways of extending love. Since he had been unable to move for quite some time, I took this as a significant sign.

For one week, he was only able to open his eyes and I gazed into their cerulean blue depths. So much can be said without words between soulmates.

The night before his passage, I received a call from my friend, Ellen, who had a message for me. She had been tucking her five-year-old daughter in bed and asked her, "Please say a prayer for Mommy's friend Michael who is sick in the hospital."

Kaitlyn turned her innocent little face heavenward and whispered, "God, Mommy's friend Michael is dying. Will you bring him back?"

Now recall that Ellen never used the word dying. Kaitlyn listened carefully and then turned to her mother and told her, "God said yes."

Naturally I took that to mean that we would see a miracle and that Michael would survive this ordeal. The next morning I discovered the true intent of that message. After exhausting every medical method, a doctor approached me and asked me to make the most difficult decision I have ever faced, but one that was no choice at all. He assured me that Michael would feel no pain as they turned off the machines and medications that had sustained him for the past forty days and nights. God indeed brought Michael back, enveloped in the love of all who stood with him in the room and the doctors and nurses that stood vigil with us outside the door. At the moment his heart ceased its beating, I was filled with an immense amount of love, as if all I had poured into Michael during those anguished days and nights was being poured back into me. Just the night before, I had told him that if he wanted to fight on, I would be at his side, but if he needed to go, our son Adam and I would be all right. I believe he needed that permission to relinquish his wounded body.

After they took away the machines and IVs that stood in the way, I found myself able to hug him for the first time in five and a half weeks. His body was still warm and it was as if he was hugging me back. Do you have any idea what a gift that was?

And now I write, ensconced in Michael's office on the second floor of our home. It is here that I feel him most strongly, among his stuffed animals, colorful hats, fanciful wall hangings, and a sign that reads "Imaginarium" on the door. I have promised him two things: that I will raise Adam to be a good man, and that I will use my communication skills to educate people about the vital importance of organ donation. When Michael died, he was enrolled as a seminary student on his way to ordination as an Interfaith Minister. As simple as breathing came my decision to continue his studies and become ordained in his place. We have been a team for twelve years and will continue to be so. Although I miss him achingly in body and long to hug him, I know that he is my strength in Heaven and I am his voice here on Earth. I called him Dancing Bear. Now I know he is dancing with angels.

⑨ *Edie Weinstein-Moser*

Daisy
. . . .

MY BELOVED HUSBAND Peter died in 1988. We had been married forty-one years. Peter was my best friend and we had a wonderful life, traveling, hiking, and going on adventures. The only sad part of our relationship was that we were not able to have children. I filled the need for mothering by teaching kindergarten for twenty years. I retired in 1980 so Peter and I could travel.

Peter filled the need for fathering by raising and showing prize golden retrievers. He loved the dogs, took excellent care of them, and expertly trained them. He took great pride in going to dog shows and having his dogs go through their routines. He raised several field champion dogs. One dog, whom we lovingly called Daisy at home, went on to become the "Best of Breed." Peter was very proud of her, as if she were his daughter.

Shortly after Daisy won this highest honor, Peter died of a sudden heart attack. Since Peter had been the center of my world, I was having difficulty coping. I gave all Peter's dogs away, except for Daisy, because she had been Peter's favorite. I wasn't fond of dog shows so I retired her from the ring and she became my pet. Daisy was my only comfort. My grief was so huge, I could hardly make it out of bed in the morning. But Daisy needed to be walked and needed to be fed and played with. The simple routine around her care gave my day much needed structure and purpose.

Three years passed in this way. My loneliness grew and grew. I started talking to Daisy and, in her sweet way, she would put her head on my lap and listen. I told her how much I missed Peter and how lonely I was for a companion. I was sixty-five years old and didn't even dare hope to find another partner. I had gray hair, was slightly overweight, and didn't have an outgoing personality. I assumed I would spend the rest of my life alone. I had tried going to a singles event, but felt very out of place and never wanted to go again.

In desperation, I placed a personal ad in a local paper. I was so freaked out by what I had done that I didn't answer the phone for two weeks. After that I resigned myself to living a lonely, single life.

Daisy was my only real companion. Our favorite time of day was our walks. Peter had trained Daisy so carefully that she walked right by my side. When I told her to stop or sit, she did so instantly. She was an almost perfect dog, but she did have one annoying habit. When I wasn't looking she liked to lie down in mud puddles. She loved the feel of the cool mud and water on her body. That meant hours of baths and grooming for me. She looked so happy in those puddles, though, that I had to smile in spite of myself.

One day I was walking along deep in thought, not paying much attention to Daisy. I was missing Peter so much and the beautiful life we had together. Tears came to my eyes and I found myself asking Peter to help me in my loneliness. I was so lost in my sadness that I didn't even notice Daisy had run away from me.

Finally I noticed and yelled, "Daisy, come!" She kept on running. She had never disobeyed me. I yelled again, "Daisy, stop!"

She continued to run as if a higher authority were calling her. I ran after her. Suddenly she stopped by a man walking the opposite way. He knelt down to pet her and was still petting her when I caught up. I felt annoyed with Daisy and asked the man if he had called her. He assured me he hadn't, but added that he really liked her. I reprimanded Daisy and walked on. Very reluctantly she followed me.

A week later Daisy and I were walking in an open field when she again took off, as if called by someone. Again, I yelled to her to stop and again she ignored me. As a champion field dog, this type of behavior was highly unusual. Daisy was trained to listen to commands.

Again I took off after her and stopped short when I saw where she was headed. The same man was walking toward us. This time we both laughed at the coincidence. We talked for a few minutes and I learned that he was seventy years old, recently widowed, and having difficulty coping with his grief.

My shyness overcame me and I called Daisy to continue our walk. Again she very reluctantly followed me.

Three months passed. Daisy and I walked every day and she did not run from me. The other two incidences were forgotten. Then one day, we were walking down a city street when Daisy carefully crossed the street by herself and took off running down the opposite way. Again she didn't listen when I yelled, "Stop!" I was very upset as I ran after her. Sure enough, Daisy had run to the same man.

This time, when I approached, he smiled at me and said, "I think your dog likes me." I was so amazed by what had happened that I couldn't speak. We were standing by a cafe and he asked me to join him for coffee. With Daisy happily lying at my feet, Arthur and I talked for hours. Arthur began to join me on my walks with Daisy. Our friendship blossomed and a year later we were married.

Daisy never ran from my side again. I often reflect on what made her run. Perhaps she heard the call of her beloved master, Peter, directing me out of my loneliness.

℘ *Christine Jones*

The Magic Penny

. . . .

MICHAEL WAS COMPLETELY devoted to me and to his five children. Our youngest was two years old when he died. He had bravely fought his brain cancer for seven months. He wanted to live. When he realized he was dying, he spent his remaining days preparing his family for his absence. He very much wanted the children and I to feel that his love would always be with us. He wrote letters to me and to the children to be read at special times in our lives. For instance, there was a letter to our boys to be read when they became interested in girls. He called one of his male friends who promised we would never be without firewood. Michael thought of so many things to help us during and after his passing.

He remained at home surrounded by our love toward the end of his life. On the day of his death, Halloween Day, 1996, we knew it would be soon because of his labored breathing. After the children left for school, I sat quietly with Michael and gently told him he could go whenever he felt ready. He lay there clinging to life as if he were waiting for something. The day passed very slowly. Finally, at three in the afternoon, our ten and twelve-year-old boys got home. They both came into the house and marched into the room where Michael lay. They each had a chance to hug and kiss him. Within minutes he breathed his last breath. He had been waiting to say good-bye to the children. His love filled our hearts as he departed.

So many uncanny events marked the period of time following Michael's death that I really learned not to question or analyze them, but rather to simply receive them as precious gifts. The entire period of his illness and the year that followed were marked by what felt like showers of holy water—incredible coincidences and stunning series of events unfolding in such ways as to be powerful messages. What I have learned with complete conviction is that the death of my husband was not the end of our relationship. As I honored my own process of grief and I listened with my heart I began to really experience his presence in my life.

I remember one particular morning about one week after Michael had died. I was in my busy-take-care-of-things mode, putting things in the car as I was hurrying off to tackle the challenges that faced me. I was suddenly stopped and stilled by a profound presence of Michael. I could feel him powerfully, filling me and reminding me of my strength. There was a stunning clarity to my surroundings that accompanied this experience. I remember looking around and noticing the air, the blue sky, and a bird that was circling as it came in to perch on a tall fir tree that sits on our property line. The sense of Michael's presence was so strong that I was actually responding with the shake of my head and by saying "yes" as I took in what I experienced as messages of reassurance that everything was going to be alright.

Dreams have been powerful messengers since Michael's passing. About six months after his death, I had a vivid dream: I was at a swimming pool. Michael was with me. He was sick with cancer. He was standing in front of me asking how he looked. I remember him standing right in front of me with his swim trunks and his bare chest. He had a penny embedded in his chest. I noticed it and wondered how it got there. The penny was directly over his heart and it was very shiny, as if it had a coating of varnish on it. He asked me if he should try to get it out of there. I replied, "No, just leave it there. It might be good luck." This was a very clear dream, but it didn't stay in my conscious mind as it didn't seem significant. It was just tucked into my dream log and filed away.

About one month later, I began to notice pennies lying around. I had forgotten my dream but I kept coming upon pennies. They would be lying here and there. It started gradually and increased finally to a point that I had to take notice—by then I was finding eight to twelve pennies each day. They were always single pennies. This had become something I could no longer ignore. I finally put one of them on a special sculpture that sits in my bedroom. I also wrote a paragraph in my journal about finding all these pennies.

A couple of days later, a series of events unfolded that brought the dream to my conscious mind. My journal entry from that day, written before noon, was: "Read a pamphlet on grief and bereavement this morning which cautions against using alcohol, drugs, excessive work, and 'magical thinking' as a way of avoiding grief." The term "magical thinking" jumps out at me. I find it offensive. I ponder how so many judgments and assumptions about life exist and I think of how truly magical life actually is. Life is so much richer and deeper than we are typically open to. I wish to challenge myself to continue opening, seeing more and more, judging less and less. What some may term as "magical thinking" can actually be sacred material.

"Today I have already come across two pennies, single pennies lying blatantly in the center of my path. Simple yet powerful messages of hope, faith, and trust in this holy process."

My journaling then continues (written at bedtime): "I ended up calling Glo in the early half of the day. I shared with her the irritation that I felt when I read the pamphlet on grief. It felt good to share with her as she understands me. I also tell her about all the pennies I keep finding and how I am just receiving these as messages of hope and faith.

"Later in the afternoon I am frantically packing for our trip to Inverness. I lean over to pick up some clothes off the floor when I am suddenly struck with the realization of my dream about Michael with the penny embedded in his chest. I am thrilled right down to my bones and goosebumps appear up and down my arms. I bathe in the incredibly beautiful power with which this is speaking to me. I again call Glo and share with her what an incredible experience I have just had. She remembers my dream about the penny in Michael's chest, as I had shared it with her back when I had it."

What is a penny? It is the smallest denomination of currency, but in great numbers it can accumulate into vast monetary wealth. It is a symbol of the little gifts in life, the ordinary happenings, which we can either ignore or accept into our lives as magical gifts, which will accumulate into vast spiritual wealth. Why was the penny in the center of Michael's chest? It was over his heart, drawing my attention to the simple, ordinary gifts that come from the heart, the magic of loving and receiving love from others.

I have again received a profound gift and I am reminded to stay open, keep listening, trusting, and being as alive as I can be. Life is truly steeped with so much meaning, and when I trust I find no need to analyze. I pray to open and continue to grow deeper and deeper in love.

℗ *Cindy Lou Rowe*

Loving Arms

. . . .

I'LL NEVER FORGET the day my husband, Todd, was diagnosed with cancer. I was in a state of shock. Neither of us
thought he would ever get sick. I was the one who seemed
more frail in my body and Todd was the one who usually took
care of me.

Over the next two years as he battled his illness, I battled it
with him. We even thought we had it licked at one point, but it
came back, and with a vengeance. Finally my gallant Todd was
bedridden, a mere shadow of the man I once knew.

He seemed to take it all in stride, at least when he wasn't in
too much pain. It got to the point where my full-time job was
taking care of my husband. Todd wasn't much of a talker but,
right before he lost his ability to talk, I broached the subject of
him dying. I told him I never wanted to hold him back if he
needed to go on. He thanked me for saying that, but said it
wasn't his time yet. He said he would let me know. Shortly
after that he couldn't talk anymore, and seemed more peaceful.

I felt the time for his dying was close. He was pitifully thin
and his breathing didn't come easily. Each night I went to bed
and prayed for God to be merciful and take my beloved husband home. Each morning there he was, still hanging on to life
by a thread.

I gave myself fully to my labor of love, the work of caring
for a dying husband. Although I had the help of visiting nurses
and aides during the day, I wanted to be the main person taking care of him. Weeks went by. I grew more and more tired.

One day, one of the nurses asked me why Todd was holding on so tightly to life. But I didn't know either.

It became harder and harder for me to take care of Todd. I found myself wishing he would die. I hated having those thoughts. It seemed so selfish of me. But I felt so spent, I couldn't help it.

Then one night I had a dream that Todd was taking care of me. He was strong again. I felt so happy in the dream, to finally be taken care of. It was so vivid that I remembered it first thing in the morning. I went downstairs to the living room where my sick husband lay in his hospital bed. He always seemed happy to see me but, because he could barely move, it was difficult for him to show it. Standing there over him, the feeling of the dream almost overwhelmed me. I was so very much needing to feel taken care of by him. I hardly had anything left of the care-giver in me. If only he could hold me just one more time.

I don't know what came over me to do what I did next, but all I know is I felt utterly compelled to climb into the bed on top of my husband. I could no longer be the caregiver. I felt like a little girl needing her daddy's love, needing to feel safe in her daddy's arms. It didn't even matter that my weight might be too much for his frail body.

I didn't expect Todd to do anything. I knew how weak he was. But I knew what I was needing. I started to relax. It felt so good, just like in the dream. Then very slowly his arms, which had not moved in weeks, came up weakly around my back. My husband was actually holding me! I felt so small then, and Todd so big and powerful. I could hardly believe it was happening. I felt so complete.

A moment later, Todd took his last breath, a faint smile on his face. He could finally let go. And I finally understood why. He needed one last time of giving his love to me. Before he died, he needed to be strong for me. He needed to die in character and with integrity. And I needed this caring from him one last time, so it could be permanently imprinted in my memory.

In the years since Todd's death, it has brought me such comfort to remember the feeling of those loving, fatherly arms surrounding me. There have been days I felt I could hardly go on, but then I close my eyes and feel again the sensation of being held by arms so humanly weak but so divinely strong. Those arms are ever around me, every minute of every day.

⊗ Marianne Abraham

Mr. Lincoln's Rose

· · · · · · · · · · · · · · · · · · · ·

I HAD FORTY-NINE wonderful years with my husband, Daniel. We met when we were twenty-one-year-old college students. I knew Daniel was my life partner after just a few dates. We were engaged and married within the year.

We had our ups and downs, but our commitment to being together grew steadily. We had four children within four years, a boy, twin girls, and another boy. You can just imagine how busy we were! Daniel was a wonderful father, and eventually grandfather. Everything he did he seemed to do very well, but he especially excelled at being the best husband and friend I could ever imagine.

Daniel retired from teaching five years after our last child left home. What followed were ten wonderful years of spending every day together. We liked to hike and canoe, but our favorite activity was gardening. We loved creating beautiful gardens and felt closest to God when we were out among the flowers, vegetables, and roses.

We grew a little of everything, but our favorite was roses. We both loved to fuss over the rose bushes as if they were fine ladies and gentlemen needing to be pampered. We put the best organic fertilizers around the stems and rejoiced with each bloom. We called them all by name and were very fond of each one. I know this must sound silly, but we had a relationship with each bush.

Though we loved them all, our favorite rose bush was our Mr. Lincoln. Mr. Lincoln produced the most fragrant red blooms imaginable. It was always cause for celebration when Mr. Lincoln produced his first rose of the season. We would cut it and ceremoniously carry it into the house to be put in a place of honor. For days we would ooh and ahh over the rose as it filled our home with fragrance. Mr. Lincoln's last bloom usually came around the end of October. The other bushes had all stopped producing by then, so his bloom was cause for much nostalgia. We'd cut the rose and bring it to our table and enjoy it even while the petals fell. Then we knew we'd have to wait until April for another.

The last ten years we had together were very beautiful. We greatly enjoyed each other's company. When the winter rains and cold would keep us inside, Daniel would read to me. We didn't like watching TV or movies and preferred the quiet of a comfortable corner where Daniel would read. Sometimes he read to me from gardening books; sometimes he'd pick a biography of a great person, and sometimes we would get engrossed in a mystery. It didn't matter what he read, I just loved sitting there and listening to his soothing and compassionate voice.

Daniel complained of some pains in his chest, but we didn't think much of them. One evening toward the end of October, he had a massive heart attack and died before the paramedics could get to our remote country house. I didn't even have a chance to say good-bye.

The next morning I walked out in the garden. Mr. Lincoln had produced his last rose of the season that morning. "This is for Daniel," I thought. I picked the rose and brought it into the house, placing it by my favorite picture of my beloved.

Daniel was my mate for life. His absence was a great loss to me. We were always side by side in every aspect of life. So, in the time after his passing, I felt totally alone. My children and grandchildren were very supportive and all wanted me to stay at their houses so I wouldn't feel so alone. I preferred to be alone in my home. It was here I could best remember my husband.

The winter was long and hard that year. Nights would find me sitting in Daniel's chair, reading to myself. The sadness and grief of my loss grew stronger and stronger, like a choking weed in our beloved garden. "If only I knew that Daniel was close to me now," I sadly thought, "Then I would be able to bear the pain and loneliness."

Finally one February night, I cried out asking for assurance that Daniel was close. My heart was breaking from my loss. I wiped my tears and sat in Daniel's chair, remembering every special quality about him. Suddenly I began to smell the very faint fragrance of a Mr. Lincoln rose.

"That's odd," I thought, "I must be imagining this."

I got up and walked around our house. It was cold and rainy outside and there were no flowers anywhere in the house. I returned to Daniel's chair and the scent grew stronger, making it clear that this was definitely not my imagination. I felt myself surrounded by the fragrance of Mr. Lincoln's finest roses.

Then I knew that, without a doubt, this was Daniel's way of letting me know he was still close to me. Of course, I smiled to myself, what a perfectly logical way for Daniel to let his presence be known to me! It was, after all, our favorite scent. My beloved husband and dearest friend had never left me. He is by my side, loving me still.

The amazing thing is that the scent of Mr. Lincoln's roses stayed in our home for a full week. My children all came and smelled for themselves and received a reassurance of their dad's presence. After our last child had come and smelled the fragrance, the scent gradually faded as mysteriously as it had come.

℘ *Margaret Williams*

Acknowledgments

We wish to thank Mary Jane Ryan, our editor at Conari Press, for sharing our feelings about the tremendous spiritual forces behind all relationships. It was often her tears on the manuscript pages that became her seal of approval for a good story.

Thank you, everyone at Conari, for working together to bring more light to the world.

Thanks to our personal assistant, Tracy Wikander, not only for entering part of this book into the computer and helping us in the office, but also for contributing her own story of meeting her husband, David ("My Vow").

We thank our children, Rami, Mira, and John-Nuri, for giving us some very practical feedback about some of the stories.

About the Authors

· ·

Joyce and Barry Vissell have been a couple since 1964. A nurse and medical doctor/psychiatrist, their main interest since 1972 has been counseling and teaching. As a result of the interest in their books, they travel internationally, conducting talks and workshops on relationship, parenting, and personal growth. They are the founders and directors of the Shared Heart Foundation, a nonprofit organization dedicated to relationship and family life as a spiritual path. Joyce and Barry Vissell write a monthly column, "New Dimensions of Relationship," for newspapers and magazines worldwide. It covers many timely topics about relationship and spirituality that have not been addressed in their books. They live with their three children, Rami, Mira, and John-Nuriel, four golden retrievers, four cats, and one horse at their home and center on a hilltop near Santa Cruz, California, where they counsel individuals and couples, and offer classes, workshops, and training programs.

Other books and tapes by Joyce and Barry Vissell include:

The Shared Heart: Relationship Initiations and Celebrations
Models of Love: The Parent-Child Journey
Risk To Be Healed: The Heart of Personal and Relationship Growth
The Heart's Wisdom: A Practical Guide to Growing Through Love
The Shared Heart Experience
    (two hour video workshop)
Four Paths to the Heart
    (audio cassette of guided visualizations)
Shared Heart Cards (oracle card set)
The Shared Heart Tape: The Relationship of Love
    (audio cassette)
The Journey of Love: Couples Moving into Parenthood (audio cassette)
Mother-Child Bonding During Pregnancy (audio cassette)
Transitions into Fatherhood: Personal Growth for Expectant Fathers (audio cassette)

And by their daughter, Rami:
Rami's Book: The Inner Life of a Child

For more information about the work of the Vissells or the Shared Heart Foundation, you can receive a free (biannual) heartletter from them, including information about workshops or events with them to be held in your area, and more information about their books, video workshop, and audiotapes. If you have a true miracle story or know someone who does, Joyce and Barry will consider it for a future book. They may be contacted through:

The Shared Heart Foundation
P. O. Box 2140
Aptos, California 95001
1-800-766-0629 (locally 831-684-2299)
www.sharedheart.org
vissell@cruzio.com

"MEANT TO BE" STORY CONTEST

Are you now or have you ever been in a relationship that was meant to be? We invite you to submit your own story of miraculous love. The authors will select the most amazing story as the contest winner. Winner will receive a weekend workshop with Joyce and Barry Vissell. Plus, all entries will be considered for a sequel to this book.

Send your miraculous love story to Joyce and Barry Vissell, P.O. Box 2140, Aptos, California, 95001, or e-mail them at vissell@cruzio.com. Contest deadline is August 1, 2000.

CONARI PRESS, established in 1987, publishes books on topics ranging from psychology, spirituality, and women's history to sexuality, parenting, and personal growth. Our main goal is to publish quality books that will make a difference in people's lives—both how we feel about ourselves and how we relate to one another.

Our readers are our most important resource, and we value your input, suggestions, and ideas. We'd love to hear from you—after all, we are publishing books for you!

To request our latest book catalog, or to be added to our mailing list, please contact:

CONARI PRESS

2550 Ninth Street, Suite 101
Berkeley, California 94710-2551
800-685-9595   510-649-7175
fax: 510-649-7190   e-mail: conari@conari.com
www.conari.com